# Witnesses to Calvary

# Witnesses to Calvary:

## Reflections on the Seven Last Words of Jesus

### Father Richard C. Antall

Our Sunday Visitor Publishing Division
Our Sunday Visitor, Inc.
Huntington, Indiana 46750

Our Sunday Visitor Publishing Division
Our Sunday Visitor, Inc.
200 Noll Plaza
Huntington, IN 46750

ISBN:0-87973-340-3
LCCCN: 99-75030

Cover design by Rebecca Heaston
Illustrations by Robert F. McGovern
Edited by Lisa Grote
PRINTED IN THE UNITED STATES OF AMERICA

For My Father

Richard C. Antall, Sr.

Requiescat in Pacem

# Table of Contents

# INTRODUCTION

# The Seven Last Words

Once upon a time, the two most famous women of the world died within days of each other. One was a nun who had dedicated herself to working with the poor; the other was a princess. Among the many things reported about their deaths and funerals were the last words the two reportedly said. The tabloids reported that the princess died saying, "O my God," and "Get away," this last to the paparazzi that tried to photograph her agony. The nun, according to her fellow sisters, died with the name of Jesus on her lips. If both reports are true, we can see why last words are sometimes so illuminating. The frightened princess fought for her privacy right to the moment of death. The nun died invoking her Lord.

Since classical times, the dying words of individuals have been recorded and meditated upon. They are considered revelatory and somehow essential for the understanding of a person. They allow the great ones to have their last say, and at the same time say something to us about the mortality in which we are all equal. We respect the dead in the custom of preserving their last words, but inevitably we are drawn to think about what we might say in similar circumstances.

We sometimes joke about "famous last words," but they are quite a study in themselves. We have all perhaps heard of some of them. They are supposed to offer us often-dramatic insight to great people. Plato says that Socrates' last words had to do with his pious wish to offer a sacrifice to the god Asculepius. The poet Goethe famously said, "Mehr licht!" "More light!" as he lay dying, and it has been taken as symbolic of a search for meaning.

Of course, in many cases, the insight we seek might be an illusion. There are those who say that Goethe was just asking for someone to open the shutters of a window in the dark room. Sometimes the irony is intentional, however. Alexander the Great said before he expired, "I am dying with the help of too many physicians." St. Thomas More's last words referred in jest to the beard he had grown as a prisoner in the Tower of London. As he pushed his beard off the block on which he had to lay his neck, the saint said, "This has not offended the king."

Not all the last words we remember are those of famous people. The last communications of family and friends often have great importance for us. I was ordained all of one month and a week when my father died. The last conversation that I remember having with my father was on the subject of why I could spend so much time at home. I told him that the pastor had told me to take the morning Mass and go home to be with the family. "Well, as far as work goes, it sounds like you've got it made," said my father. It is the last thing I can recall him saying to me as the cancer whittled down his life.

I was standing in line once at airport immigration and heard a woman talking about her brother's death. "He held my hand and said to me, 'Sister, I love you, and I know that you love me.' I feel such peace to know that I had a brother who loved me and who knew I loved him. Despite the sadness, he had a beautiful death." All I heard was this smidgen of conversation, and yet I could understand how significant the words of her brother had been to this most loyal sister.

These personal examples should make it easy for us to see why the Last Words of Jesus have a special importance for the believer. St. Augustine said that the cross was Christ's greatest *cathedra*.[1] For Bishop Fulton Sheen, the Last Words of Jesus were a sermon as important as the Sermon on the Mount. The meditations which make up this book are an attempt to listen to the last sermon of Jesus, His preaching from the cross.

It is not a sermon that can be followed in any one Gospel. The seven pronouncements of Jesus within it (each called a "Word") are scattered throughout the four Gospels. St. Matthew and St. Mark report Jesus saying only one thing, the moving and very troubling initial words of Psalm 22, "My God, my God, why have you forsaken me?" St. Matthew also records "[Jesus] cried out in a loud voice" one more time, but does not tell what he said. St. Luke has three Last Words of Jesus: "Father, forgive them, for they know not what they do"; "This day you shall be with me in paradise"; and "Father, into your hands I commend my spirit." St. John has the remaining three Words: "Woman, behold your son. Son, behold your mother"; "I thirst"; and "It is completed."

Three of the Words were prayers to the Father, one Word was shared by the Beloved Disciple and the Blessed Mother, another was for the Good Thief, and two seem to be quite general comments. The order of the Words, as they are examined here, is a traditional one first seen in some medieval German sermons. The devotional use of the Words seems to date from the same time.

The first time I was aware that there was a special devotion involving the Last Words of Christ was on a hot afternoon in the mission where I served as a priest for almost eight years, Immaculate Conception Parish in La Libertad, El Salvador. I was called down to the office to find the parish secretary talking to an old man.

"He wants the Seven Last Words and we don't have them," she said.

The man was obviously a *campesino*, the name is the equivalent of "farmer" and comes from the word *campo*, which means "country." Such people in El Salvador often show vestiges of the indigenous culture and are sometimes so careful about what they share that they are nearly inscrutable. This man was certainly not easy to read. His eyes stared at me with determination. I had the impression that he expected some kind of a disagreement about this question, but was prepared to be patient. He was old and his hair was white. His short body had the permanent stoop of those who have worked too hard, too long. His cowboy hat was in his hands.

I asked him what exactly he wanted. He wanted a copy of the Seven Last Words of Jesus Christ. He did not expatiate on the topic, but waited for my reply. I had never seen them on a holy card, I told him, but I would be happy to copy them out for him. Yes, that would be fine. He needed them written out.

I'm not certain that the man could read. Sometimes people who cannot read have a great respect for words, both memorized and written. I knew that many Salvadorans carry a copy of the Magnificat in their wallets as a kind of devotion or sign of protection. I presumed that the old man was going to carry the Seven Last Words in his wallet, too. I thought that perhaps he had been told that having the prayer on his person would help him.

There is much superstition in El Salvador, and many magical practices. At the time the *campesino* visited me, I didn't realize that the *brujos* of El Salvador have a twisted sort of respect for the Seven Last Words. The *brujos* practice magic, in the form of healings, findings, and spells. Some elements of their practices are natural medicine, others are remnants of an indigenous religion, and all involve some measure of cleverness. The *brujos* are good psychologists, and make astute use of symbols.

Only recently I heard from a woman who told me that she had cut up a piece of paper with the Seven Last Words printed on it in Latin and mixed it with her husband's supper. It was supposedly a remedy for his roving eye and propensity to drink. "It didn't work," she said with disappointment. I wondered if that was why she told me. Magical thinking is idolatry, but sometimes has something of innocence about it — an innocence of desperation.

There is also in some magical thinking a perverse kind of recognition of the truth. What Words of Jesus could be more important than those He said while dying on the cross? That is the grain of truth behind the distorted respect the *brujos* have for the Seven Last Words. Maybe the old *campesino* had a bit of that in him. There's a chance that he wanted some kind of talisman, or maybe the little paper was going to be a garnish for someone's supper.

He offered to pay for the little piece of paper I gave him, and only shrugged when I said that was not necessary. I will nevertheless always be grateful to him, because he made me look at the Seven Words as particularly worthy of interest.

Sometimes a dirty window is the only one with a view. That is my perhaps simplistic view of some of the popular religion in Latin America. There is a tremendous lack of clarity about its symbols sometimes, but they are such basically important symbols that the solution has to be to rescue and purify them, not throw them out. The pope has just spoken out again, in his exhortation to the Church in America, about the importance of popular piety. He, as well as the bishops in several Latin American meetings and synods, believes that in the traditional devotional life of the people there are many opportunities to meet the Lord.

Popular religion in Latin America has some classical and mystical currents. The liberation theologian Segundo Galilea was certainly correct to say, in his book *The Future of Our Past*, that the future of spirituality here is in some ways the treasure of the past. Galilea comments on the fact that popular devotions are so tied up with the humanity of Christ and why this is so important. He points out that St. Teresa of Ávila recounts in her autobiography that one of her greatest mistakes spiritually was to think that she needed to "get beyond" the Gospel stories to some more abstract sense of the divine. Christ's humanity, from His birth in the stable to His last breath on the cross, is our way to God, the only way to God.

This perception is expressed in countless ways in popular Catholicism, from breast-feeding Madonnas to the broken and tortured body of Christ on the cross. Interest in Mary and in the suffering Christ are constants in spirituality which emphasize our connection with the Divine Savior. The details of His humanity make for a bridge to His divinity. We can understand Him, and this helps us to believe that He can understand us. The pious imagination which can "connect" with a living, breathing Jesus, which hangs on His Words and stares at His suffering, is what living faith is about.

Such popular devotions sometimes clash with North American sensibility. Although we have no trouble with people torturing themselves for athletic achievement ("no pain, no gain"), we do have difficulty connecting our spiritual life with physical suffering. We must remember that it is not necessarily pessimistic to reflect on suffering. Sometimes it is the opposite of optimism to ignore the pain of this world. Confronting problems often brings strength, and so it is in prayer, also. Taking into account the suffering of this world represented and recapitulated on the cross of Christ can be liberating.

My experience in El Salvador taught me this truth especially. The insight connecting our life and suffering with the Gospels was what led me to write my first book of meditations, *The Way of Compassion*, a book about the Seven Sorrows of Mary. Both that book and this one have seven parts. Besides the numerical coincidence, the books are alike in that they are the fruit of meditation that took me to the foot of the cross. I think that seeing the desperate conditions of life among the rural poor in El Salvador has helped me understand a bit more the sufferings of Christ.

I served in the mission of my diocese in El Salvador from 1986 to 1993. In 1998, my bishop gave me the opportunity to return to the mission. I had been back in El Salvador a little more than a week when I was called to visit a woman, gravely ill. Catalina was in her eighties, practically deaf, and living with a woman who had taken her in out of the kindness of her heart. Francisca, Catalina's hostess, was convinced that her boarder would soon die. It was apparently part of her intuition that Catalina might not die as soon as she could if she did not receive the last rites. Many people have the idea that a Catholic might fight on and suffer more in hopes of dying with the sacraments.

"Catalina is very Catholic. She used to read the Bible until lately; she is too tired and sick now." Francisca directed herself to the sick woman, and practically shouted, "Tell the Padre how you know the Seven Last Words."

Catalina looked at me and smiled. "Do you know the Seven Last Words?" she asked.

"They tell me you know them," I said. This was successfully communicated after about three tries.

"Say them for the Padre," said Francisca, again shouting as if to the street.

Catalina began to say them, beginning, "The Seven Last Words of Our Lord Jesus Christ." When she came to "It is completed," she said the words in Latin, "*Consumatum est.*"

I had already spoken to someone of turning my reflections on the Seven Last Words into a meditation book. Meeting Catalina was a powerful incentive to keep working on those reflections. There was something very impressive and appropriate about a dying woman repeating to herself the Words of the dying Savior. It was a lesson I will not forget. When one experiences Calvary personally, what better thing to do than to unite oneself with Christ on the cross?

No better justification for these meditations is needed.

Father Richard Antall
Parroquia Nuestra Señora de Guadalupe
Chirilagua, San Miguel
El Salvador

# PREAMBLE

■■■■■ ■ ■■■ ■■■ ■■ ■■■ ■■ ■ ■■ ■ ■ ■ ■■ ■■ ■

# Witnesses to Calvary

I have tried to place myself at the foot of the cross and to imagine what it would have been like to listen intently to what Jesus said as He was dying. There was a crowd on Calvary. It was a diverse group, with the chief priests and elders of the Jews, the Roman soldiers, the two thieves, women disciples (according to Matthew and Mark), the weeping women of Jerusalem (Luke), and the three Marys and the Beloved Disciple (according to John). In order to see Jesus on the cross in my imagination, to really hear what He is saying, I have to enter the crowd around the cross and gradually wedge my way in.

The best place to listen to Jesus would have been in the company of the three Marys and the Beloved Disciple. The Blessed Virgin Mary, Mary Magdalene, and Mary of Clopas were there, according to John's Gospel. We know practically nothing about Mary of Clopas except that her husband might have been one of the disciples that Jesus encountered on the way to Emmaus after His Resurrection. Mary the mother of Jesus, Mary Magdalene, and John are the three people most often depicted in the art of the passion and death of Jesus.

I concentrate on these three most familiar witnesses at the foot of the cross. I was inspired to do this by an idea I encountered in reading the great German theologian Hans Urs von Balthasar. He insisted in some of his writings on the importance of situating Jesus within the group of people who surrounded Him during His earthly ministry. Urs von Balthasar called this grouping "the human constellation of Jesus." No human life can be taken wholly apart from other people. Nor can Jesus be understood without reference to His mother, His disciples, His friends, and His enemies.

Human life is a group dynamic. We are always influencing one another in many ways, both positively and negatively. A person is revealed not so much in himself or herself, but as he or she relates to others. Even in private communications, like a diary, there is a sense of dialog with the other. Applying this human dynamic to understanding Jesus enables us to see the other people in the Gospel stories as valuable witnesses to what the Lord is like in relationship to others. A Catholic will quickly see how this reaches to our belief in the communion of the saints. Holiness for us is interrelationship.

This allows us to enter actively into the Gospel story following the method of prayer that St. Ignatius of Loyola referred to as contemplation. We imagine that we are there experiencing the event that we consider. Therefore, St. John, the Blessed Virgin Mary, and St. Mary Magdalene and their relationship to the dying Jesus are central to these reflections. I have tried to imagine the three as they have been portrayed symbolically. The Blessed Virgin presented in spiritual communion with her Son, dying with Him, almost. The Beloved Disciple, as a youth, the symbol of innocence and loyalty, learning as he suffered the lesson of his Lord's passion on Calvary. Mary Magdalene, for me, is the portrait of repentance. In these meditations I try to see and hear Jesus through their eyes and ears.

Bishop Fulton Sheen, in his sermon on the Seven Last Words, said that the three witnesses — Mary Magdalene, John, and the Blessed Virgin — represented "penitence, priesthood, and innocence:

the three types of souls to be found forever beneath the cross of Christ." I came across this classic treatment after I had prepared an essay on how the Blessed Virgin Mary might have heard the Seven Last Words. Sheen made me think of the three as coordinates with which I could map out the meaning of the Last Words. The three who stood at the foot of the cross were a constellation of persons who loved Jesus, and whose faces would be His only human consolation in His last agony.

The Last Words in my interpretation of them resonate differently in each of the three. I can only imagine what each of the three could have felt, thought, or prayed at the foot of the cross. While these meditations are a kind of speculation, they are based on the human reality of perspective. We always hear things according to our own experience, and I have taken the descriptions of the three offered by Bishop Sheen —penitence, priesthood, and innocence — as trajectories of my thought.

Tradition has associated Mary Magdalene with what appear to be several different women mentioned in the Gospels. *The Golden Legend*, the great medieval book of saints, identified Mary Magdalene as the sister of Martha and Lazarus and also as the woman who washed the feet of Jesus with her tears and dried them with her hair. Current scholarship distinguishes Mary Magdalene from the other two women, but sometimes goes even further.

Some scholars no longer see her even as a symbol of repentance. St. Luke says that the Lord cured Mary Magdalene of seven devils (Lk 8:2), but now some think this a reference to some sort of nervous disorder, like epilepsy. This seems to me to be a rather fundamentalist reading of the text. Its exclusive identification of demons with disease is simplistic. The thinking goes like this: the saint had seven devils, and devils were associated with illness; therefore, Mary Magdalene was very ill indeed, because she had seven of them.

How would this interpretation deal with the saying of Jesus in Matthew 12:43-45? An unclean spirit leaves a man and roams about the desert. When he decides to return to "his house," as he calls the man, he finds the place clean. Therefore, he joins forces with seven other spirits "more wicked than itself" and the result is that "the final condition of that man is worse than the first" (Mt 12:45).

Can we believe that Jesus was speaking in this passage as some sort of neurological clinician? It is obvious that there is a moral sense to the "final condition" of the unfortunate person now occupied with the seven evil spirits. There is even the implication of moral struggle in the idea that the unclean spirit needed reinforcements when he discovered that the man was clean.

I like to think of the symmetry of the Seven Words with the seven demons. Mary Magdalene had suffered seven wounds and the Last Words were seven remedies. Her penitence — the transformation in her because of her experience of Christ — brought her to the cross, and then led her to the empty tomb. She had already experienced a rising to new life, and thus was an excellent choice to be the first witness to Christ's Resurrection.

The Beloved Disciple has been identified with the author of the Gospel of John, I, II, and III John, and the Book of Revelation. Many Scripture scholars have debated whether "John, the son of Zebedee" is the same person as the Beloved Disciple. This is obviously a serious problem for scholars, but it does not concern us here. The name of the disciple is not important. What is essential is the idea of a follower of Jesus who knew the Lord intimately, and his experience of the Seven Words. As a priest, I have felt a personal identification with the disciple at the foot of the cross. That identification and various themes of the writings of John have nourished my meditations from this perspective.

The Blessed Virgin Mary was the mother of Jesus, and in these meditations I have meditated on her motherhood as a spiritual path. Mary is always a special way to connect with the reality of the humanity of Christ. In the relationship between Jesus and Mary there is something of the most elemental stuff of our lives. Her human experience of her Son, secret and profoundly intimate, was also her life of grace and her relationship to God. She loved God by feeding Him, clothing Him, rocking Him in her arms at night. She loved Him by worrying about Him, following Him, and watching Him die. It is impossible to plumb the depths of that kind of experience of God, but it is certainly edifying to try.

I am grateful to God for the prayer that resulted in this book. It took me a while to write it; there were false starts and periods in which I would have rather thought or written about many other things. But I kept coming back to the three witnesses, and they kept making me strain to listen to the Words of the Crucified. I hope they will do the same for you.

# CHAPTER ONE

# The First Word

*When they came to the place called the Skull, there they cruci-fied him, along with the criminals — one on his right, the other on his left. Jesus said, "Father, forgive them, for they do not know what they are doing" (Lk 23:33-34).*

"Gentleman, this is not the Bible," said an Anglican bishop while he showed his clergy a copy of the King James Bible; "it is only a translation." This might seem a bit pedantic, but it is true that there are some insights to be gleaned only from reference to the original. For instance, a minor point of grammar about the above reading has a great meaning for me. What is translated simply, "he said," is in the imperfect tense of the Greek. The imperfect tense is more literally translated, "he was saying," which has led some scholars to think that perhaps Jesus' prayer for the pardon of His enemies was repeated.

We repeat ourselves whenever we want to drive home a point. Can you imagine two people in love saying, "I love you," only once in their lives? If Jesus said, "Father, forgive them, for they know not what they do," more than once, it would not only justify the imper-fect tense, but also add to the human intensity of this Word.

Words of forgiveness could never have a more dramatic context. The Son of God sent to earth to redeem humankind ends up executed as an accused revolutionary. Jesus Himself told the story as that of the son of the owner of the vineyard killed by envious and ungrateful upstarts. "This is the heir; come, let us kill him, and let us seize on his inheritance" (Mt 21:38b KJV).

It was not only the killing, but also the way He was killed. St. Paul emphasized the scandal of the cross. "The message of the cross is foolishness" to those without faith, said the apostle in 1 Corinthians 1:18. The steadfast love of Jesus was evident in that He was "obedient to death, even to death on a cross" (Phil 2:8). Paul's sensitivity on the subject is reflected by an early Roman graffito of a donkey crucified which mocks Christians for adoring one who suffered such a shameful death.

The barbaric punishment of crucifixion had a long history even before Jesus. Some scholars think that crucifixion began with the Medes and Persians, but after the conquest of the Middle East by Alexander the Great crucifixion was a common feature of the Greek or Hellenistic culture. It spread west in the Mediterranean to Carthage, which most likely introduced the Romans to the practice during the Punic Wars. Only with the coming to power of the Constantine would crucifixion be banned, some three hundred years after Christ's death.

Even before Constantine, who, as a believer, ended the practice out of reverence for Jesus, civilized people were horrified by crucifixion. This probably explains why there are so few references to the cross and crucifixion in secular literature. Nevertheless, Cicero comments that crucifixion was "a most cruel and disgusting penalty." He also pronounced a strange sort of failed prophecy when he said, "The very name 'cross' should not only be far from the body of a Roman citizen, but also from his thoughts, his eyes, and his ears."

The saying echoes strangely when one thinks of Catholic Rome, with its hundreds of churches and shrines.

Other famous references to crucifixion occur in the Roman dramatist Plautus, who lived in the second century before Christ. Plautus made dark comedy of the cross in his popular plays, with slaves joking about crucifixion as their destiny. It was a kind of classical gallows humor, but premised on the idea that the cross was the ultimate disgrace.

The austere Stoic philosopher and Roman statesman Seneca, who lived from 4 BC to 65 AD, also considered the cross disgraceful, but took it most seriously. The cross, he said, was the "accursed tree."

The Jewish historian Josephus was closer to modern sensibility when he said that execution on the cross was "the most pitiable of deaths." He reports of the crucifixion of 800 prisoners by Alexander Jannacus during the first century before Christ, and of 2,000 Jews put to death by the cross in 4 BC. Crucifixion was a frightening way to die and was used as part of the psychology of terror by which the Romans maintained their empire.

Taking into account the horror of the death, we can better understand the power of Christ's Words. Imagine someone in a death camp like Auschwitz saying, "Forgive them, Father, for they know not what they are doing." The injustice and cruelty of the cross make the forgiveness that it won even more paradoxical and moving. As a prayer, this Word of Jesus has even more force because it contrasts the intimacy of Father and Son with the barbarity of the men who put the Lord to death.

The three witnesses could feel that contrast. Through the prisms they represent for us, we can see the refraction of this Word in many different lights. Their human experience can help us try to apply Christ's wisdom to our own lives. The three witnesses are bridges for our own sympathetic identification with what Jesus says. Like the edges of a prism, the edges of our experience can make Christ's light more readily visible in its manifold beauty.

## Mary Magdalene

A person forgiven is a person rescued. Victor Hugo shows this in the great novel *Les Miserables*. The hero, Jean Valjean, steals some silver plates from Bishop Bienvenu. When the gendarmes stop him, they take him to the bishop so that they can file an accusation. The bishop pretends he gave the plates to Valjean, and makes haste to give him two candlesticks which go with the set. The gift saves Valjean from another term in prison.

The bishop waits for the gendarmes to go away and then says, "Never forget that you promised me to use this money to become an honest man." There had never been such a promise. Jean Valjean does not even respond to the bishop, who continues, "My brother, you no longer belong to evil but to good. I have purchased your soul. I have taken it away from dark thoughts and the spirit of perdition and have given your soul to God."

*Les Miserables*, which was on the Church's Index of Forbidden Books because of its virulent attack on the vowed life, is actually a parable of redemption and expiation. Jean Valjean had become a criminal because of the injustice of a society that punished him with nineteen years of prison because he had stolen a loaf of bread. At first he did not know how to accept the grace of the bishop's gesture. In fact, he even feels angry at first, and in his anger, he mistreats a young child. Then enlightenment comes and Valjean becomes a new man.

Significantly, Hugo says that he adopts a new name, Monsieur Madeleine. The name is a version of Magdalene and the reference is not accidental. Bad Catholic that he was, Victor Hugo knew who could be the patron saint of repentance and leading a new life. He knew also that grace inspires grace, and Jean Valjean spends the rest of the rather long novel saving others from evil.

The bishop's forgiveness became the basis for the rest of the criminal's life. I think that something similar happened with Mary Magdalene. The forgiveness and new life she experienced in Jesus must have changed her so completely that she understood that God's mercy was everything. That is my idea of her holiness, and of all holiness, in fact.

I imagine her saying, "How like him, this forgiveness." She had experienced the same forgiveness, and she had not merited it, either. Her personal will could assent to mercy for everyone. The devotion of the Divine Mercy of Blessed Faustina apparently has the same perspective. The prayer, "In atonement of our sins and those of the whole world," indicates an alignment with God's universal love.

There is, of course, another possibility, but one not congruent to the Church's understanding of holiness. Mary Magdalene could have been attacked by the demon that wants us to withhold forgiveness of others. Jesus talked about this possibility in the parable of the unmerciful servant, the one who is forgiven a debt but cannot forgive another's. The master says to that servant, "You wicked servant, I canceled all that debt of yours because you begged me to. Shouldn't you have had mercy on your fellow servant just as I had on you?" (Mt 18:32-33).

Good people are sometimes tempted not to forgive. Jesus knew this about us and adverted to it several times. The Our Father explicitly conditions our reception of forgiveness upon our ability to forgive. We have a tendency to compartmentalize life. There is one standard for us and another for everyone else. We no sooner convert and better our lives than we begin to concentrate on the faults of others. There is a joke about immigrants that goes like this: An

Irishman walks onto the dock in New York and looks over his shoulder to say, "Look at all these foreigners coming in."

In religious discourse this would be translated as, "Look who else is lined up for God's mercy." Jesus had a parable about that, too, the one of the laborers who came late to the field but received the full day's pay anyway. Mary Magdalene had to resist that tendency which is in all of us to seek preferential treatment for ourselves. Novelist Gore Vidal commented on this when he said, "It is not enough that we succeed; others must fail."

Mary Magdalene looked upon Jesus and watched His executioners. What a tremendous perspective she had to see the work of God's mercy on the cross! Despite the horrible pain, there was mercy. Despite the even more horrifying mockery, there was forgiveness. Despite all the evil, love. God's solidarity with those who need forgiveness was a constant in the life of Jesus. Mary Magdalene discovered the truth that Dorothy Day wrote about when she said, "God is on the side even of the unworthy."

The forgiven saint at the foot of the cross can be a help to us. If we could forgive in the midst of our suffering, we would really know that we have been forgiven.

## John, the Beloved Disciple

The Beloved Disciple was the only male follower of Jesus who had the courage to be present when they crucified the Lord. But this could not have been his only suffering. He believed in Jesus and now he witnessed not only the apparent failure of the Lord's ministry but also a personal disaster. The Beloved Disciple had to be tremendously shocked at the sequence of events.

Three things especially had to have made him feel lost. First, there was his personal confidence and admiration in the Lord. Followers of great people and saints often have a trust in those people that makes it hard to believe anything bad can happen to them. The Beloved Disciple must have been horrified that this holy man whom he followed with love would be subjected to this violence. How could they do this to a prophet?

Second, it must have been difficult to believe that the principals behind the execution were the religious leaders of his own people. If we presume, as many scholars do, that the Beloved Disciple is the same disciple who takes Peter to the palace of the high priest where Jesus is interrogated and tried, that means that he knew these leaders. He appears to have been well connected to the religious establishment — he not only enters the palace but also arranges for Peter to get into the courtyard, where Peter can warm himself from the chill of the night. The Beloved Disciple was someone who had entry into the house of the high priest. How it must have astonished him that the men he knew would plot violently against Jesus.

The third thing that must have shocked the Beloved Disciple was that one of his companions in the Twelve was a party to the plot against Jesus. I imagine the "disciple whom Jesus loved" standing near the cross and remembering, as if in a dream, the events of the garden of Gethsemane when Judas came with the soldiers to take Jesus prisoner.

His Gospel does not recount the kiss of Judas and Jesus' question, "Are you betraying the Son of Man with a kiss?" (Lk 22:48), the Lord's version of Caesar's famous "Et tu, Brute?" Was it sentiment that did not permit the Beloved Disciple to go into detail about the betrayal of Jesus by Judas? Perhaps it hurt too much to remember. The Gospel of John mentions the betrayer's name three times in five verses but does not recount a face-to-face encounter between Jesus and Judas Iscariot. Instead, there is the laconic observation, "And Judas the traitor was standing there with them" (Jn 18:5).

Francis Bacon, the great English writer and scientist, observed,

"We read that we ought to forgive our enemies; but we do not read that we ought to forgive our friends." His point is that it is in fact more difficult to forgive those who have been close to us that those who were franker enemies. Betrayal is often worse than mere hostility.

The Beloved Disciple knew from the Last Supper that Judas would betray Christ. The scene, famous in so many artistic representations, of John leaning on the chest of the Lord depicts the moment the Beloved Disciple learned of the identity of the betrayer. I had not thought of this until recently: what is regarded as a gesture symbolic of intimacy with Jesus was caused by curiosity about betrayal. The juxtaposition of the confidence of the Beloved Disciple, both with the Lord and with Peter (who prompts the question "Lord, who is it who will betray you?") and Judas' duplicity is quite dramatic. I believe that it would also be intensely painful for the Beloved Disciple.

Perhaps of the three shocking elements of the experience of the crucifixion for the loyal disciple this last was the most terrible. However, the impact of all of them was not separate but was felt all at once. It is hard to think of how difficult that hour must have been at the foot of the cross. Fulton Sheen said that the Beloved Disciple represented priesthood, which is always attached to a sense of the sacred. John's priestly soul had to be engulfed in the terror of the sacrilege committed on the cross.

Recently, I heard a bishop talk about the atrocities of Rwanda, where Catholics of one tribe killed Catholics of another, sometimes in the same church where both groups had once worshiped and received Communion. The bishop had heard firsthand reports of such massacres from priests and religious on a trip he had made to the country for Catholic Relief Services some time after the slaughter had stopped.

We were a small group of people who work with the poor, sitting around a dinner table, on another continent, but something of the terror of the deeds entered all our hearts. How could they do such things in the same church where they had worshiped together? Why was it that their baptism was completely forgotten in the hurricane of tribal hatred? The bishop said with tremendous irony, "Blood was thicker than even the waters of baptism."

Something of the horror of that profanation of the churches and of the mystical body of Christ will give us insight into the terror of Calvary. How painful it must have been to witness the horror of genocide. But even the death of one innocent person is very hard to accept. When the Beloved Disciple heard Jesus' Words of forgiveness, he was experiencing the extremes of violence and mercy, hate and love. Jesus had spoken many times about forgiveness, but hearing Him pardoning those who killed Him made the Words all the more powerful.

This was another aspect of priesthood. Christ's intercession for His persecutors was part of His priesthood. He went to God with prayer for the people. The Beloved Disciple, representing the principle of priesthood, was involved in that prayer of forgiveness. This can be taken in both senses of priesthood, the general one of all the faithful and the particular participation given to deacons, priests, and bishops

In the general sense we are all a priestly people who must intercede for others in the world. We pray for all humankind, especially our enemies. The Church has for mission the sanctification of the world. The spiritual leaven of prayer is very much part of the mission of each member of the Church. A priestly people intercedes for those most in God's grace, to echo one of the prayers made popular by the movement associated with the Blessed Virgin's appearance at Fátima.

Those who have received the sacrament of orders have an even greater responsibility for offering prayer. That is why the Divine Office is obligatory for those in orders — it is the recognition of a ministry of prayer for others. The Beloved Disciple was one of those ordained to pray for others and to offer the Eucharist "in memory of [Jesus]" in the Words of the Lord at the Last Supper. He was joined to Jesus in the prayer of forgiveness in a way that required that he sacrifice even some of his own feelings. As a priest, he was called to be a minister of pardon, even pardon of this terrible sin of crucifying our Lord.

The prayer of Jesus that the Father forgive His enemies had to have an echo in the heart of the Beloved Disciple. Could he say the same prayer? Could he have the same spirit of love for the enemies of the One he loved so much? Could he forgive Judas Iscariot? That for me is the true test of mercy, both for the Beloved Disciple and for every Christian. Can we have an attitude like that of Christ about even the Judases of our lives?

I work in a country that is still recovering from years of cruel civil war. Between the years 1977 and 1992, many innocent people were killed, too many of them victims of the so-called "forces of order." The stories the survivors tell make me understand why some are slow to forgive. The desire for retribution is strong. And injustice continues.

Many of us who are disciples today are often lacking in mercy. We can profit spiritually by putting ourselves at the foot of the cross with John and hear Jesus' prayer for forgiveness. It was a tremendous lesson that Jesus was giving John. He not only was called upon to forgive Judas his betrayal, but Peter's lack of courage, the failure of the other apostles to present themselves at the cross, the actions of the leaders of his people, and the brutality of the soldiers and the crowd. Jesus expects the same from us in our lives.

There is injustice in all parts of the world. In El Salvador, however, it is less refined than in the United States. It does not mask itself so well, perhaps, as it does in developed countries. When injustice is obvious and there seems to be nothing that one can do about it, there is a feeling of powerlessness that engulfs you and presses against your heart. It makes it very hard to think about forgiveness. A very rational desire that there be responsibility for actions against the innocent and that God's forgiveness and ours be connected to true contrition can become an obstacle to mercy.

Obviously there are questions of necessary responsibility and also of true contrition, but Jesus certainly was not worried about that in this prayer. What He expressed was a disposition to intercede for the wicked. I have found such an attitude very difficult to achieve in situations of injustice. It is hard to pray that God forgive someone committing injustice. In fact, however, Jesus teaches us that there is no other way. His desire is to save us all. I feel a need to lean a bit on the shoulders of the Beloved Disciple as I pray about this. Perhaps you do, too.

## The Blessed Virgin Mary

Now we turn to the woman who most likely taught the boy Jesus to pray. The Son of God had emptied Himself, in the words of Philippians, "Who, being in very nature God, / did not consider equality with God something to be grasped" (Phil 2:6) and was obedient to Mary and Joseph. He was like us in all things but sin and "grew in wisdom and stature, and in favor with God and men" (Lk 2:52). That progress was something Mary watched and meditated on. It was something that she contributed to, as any mother does, as most of our mothers did, by teaching her child to pray.

There is a popular book of Marian reflection that talks about the "silence" of Mary. A friend of mine teased his wife about it, saying if she was "silent" what was there to write a book about? Actually, the silence makes a great deal of sense to me. With whom can you share the mystery of the virginal conception? How do you talk about holding your Creator in your arms? What do you say about the tears of the child who is the Son of God, of the way a mother cradles a divine baby to drowsiness and sleep? No one could understand the extraordinary intimacy of the Mother of God.

She now hears Him praying to God the Father. It has been some time since the relationship of Mary to the Blessed Trinity was a natural theme of preaching or discussion. But this prayer should help us consider that mystery also. She was a witness, while He lived, who knew that this man was the Son of God. She could hear His prayer in the profundity of the mystery of the love of Father and Son. Mary had accepted the plan of God the Father, had conceived the Son by the Holy Spirit. All Christians have to have a relationship with the Holy Trinity, but Mary's cannot be equaled in its intimacy.

I do not mean here the actual physical connection with Christ, the fact that her blood nourished Him in the womb, that her milk made it possible for His body to grow, that He relied on her in the thousand ways a son needs a good mother. The Lord Himself seemed to discount the merely physical intimacy when He said to the woman who spoke to Him from the crowd about His mother, "Blessed rather are those who hear the word of God and obey it" (Lk 11:28).

This does not discount the intimacy of Our Lord with His mother. It emphasizes, however, what her example especially means for us. As fellow hearers of the Word, we can imitate her. We cannot pretend to emulate her in the grace of her special vocation, only in the deep spiritual values which made her maternal relationship with Christ a spiritual one. "Blessed is she who has believed that what the Lord has said to her will be accomplished!" (Lk 1:45).

At the foot of the cross she heard more Words. She listened to the voice of her Son, but she also heard the voice of her Savior. Her Son was God's Son. And He pleaded again and again for mercy for those who killed Him.

Was she too stunned to think? I have seen many mothers "besides themselves" because of what happened to their children. Was she desperately sad, like some weeping women I have seen at the burials of the poor, whose emotion leads them to wail? Mary in sorrow has been depicted in different ways. Sometimes the artists depict her pain in her face, and sometimes her faith in God.

I think that she probably prayed to the Father along with her Son. Her life was His, and that much is clear from the way she followed Him in His pilgrimage to Calvary. The union of her soul with His was complete. Her perfect innocence was also perfect identification. Can we doubt that she would ask God for mercy, also? Centuries of Marian devotion and present-day authentic Marian prophecy have emphasized her compassion and mercy.

One of Mary's most beautiful titles is Our Lady of Mercy. Perhaps it began at Cana, when her sensitivity to the problem of the bride and groom provided the pretext for the miracle that inaugurated the kingdom. Throughout history, people have called upon her in the Hail Mary to intercede for us. For how many Christians has she been a sign of hope and the inspiration of conversion? The bishop who ordained me, now a cardinal, once told a group of us when we were seminarians that the feasts of Mary are the ones that occasion the grace of conversion in the worst of sinners.

Is that the echo of the prayer of Jesus, "Father, forgive them, for they know not what they do"? Simeon had said that a sword would pierce her heart. Is that the secret of her openness? Our religion has many violent metaphors that are transformed into images of God's love. The Sacred Heart of Jesus wounded for us by the soldier's lance. The Lamb of God, which the Apocalypse insists has been cut for sacrifice, is another example, as is the Immaculate Heart of Mary, pierced with a sword of suffering. All of these images are to remind us of the radical openness of the two Hearts, as some Marian theology frames the question.

We talk about our own hearts being broken, as if they did not match the tensile strength of pressure upon them. But who would deny that some of the so-called broken-hearted have better hearts than ours? The Scripture indicates that Mary's heart was cut through, a terribly violent image, but also one that indicates her special role of cooperation in the salvation of the world.

Generations after generation of Christians have invoked her in prayer. Is her prayer such a help because she learned so much about mercy that day at the foot of the cross? We call her in the *Salve Regina*[2] "our most gracious advocate." Thinking of her reminds me of a fictional advocate, on the greatest characters that came from the pen of Shakespeare. The bard has Portia give a great speech on mercy, something many of us had to study in high school. The poetry is so true that it is worthy of the Queen of Mercy herself.

> The quality of mercy is not strained,
> It droppeth as the gentle rain from heaven
> Upon the place beneath; it is twice blessed;
> It blesses him that gives and him that takes;
> 'Tis mightiest in the mightiest; it becomes
> The throned monarch better than his crown;
> His scepter shows the force of temporal power,
> The attribute to awe and majesty,
> Wherein doth sit the dread and might of kings;
> But mercy is above the sceptred sway,
> It is enthroned in the heart of kings,
> It is the attribute of God Himself. . .

The speech, addressed to the Jew Shylock in the play *The Merchant of Venice*, ends with a great Christian message:

> Though justice be thy plea, consider this,
> That in the course of justice none of us
> Should see salvation; we do pray for mercy,
> And that same prayer doth teach us all to render
> The deeds of mercy (IV.i. 184).

Mercy, said Shakespeare, was a divine attribute. Later Alexander Pope would echo this idea in the line that has become a cliché, "To err is human; to forgive, divine."

Where is the truth of these two great poets more obvious than on the cross? The mightiest One who ever lived among our race showed His power in forgiveness. His mercy is our only hope of salvation.

Shakespeare never wrote truer words than when he said, "In the course of justice none of us should see salvation." In one of the prefaces, the Roman liturgy says the same thing, "In justice you condemned us, in mercy you redeemed us." I am convinced that one person at the foot of the cross understood this better than any of us. Meditating on her most special vocation can help us so much.

## Conclusion

We have all been at a loss for words, even in less dramatic circumstances. Jesus had no such problem. In this First Word from the cross, according to the classic ordering, He expressed His mission of forgiveness and reconciliation.

It is frightening to contemplate Calvary, the most terrible act of ingratitude in a long history of our rebellion against God, Who is a Loving Father. But it is consoling to consider this First Word to us.

We are all so limited. Our hearts are treacherous, as the prophet Jeremiah observed when he said, "Nothing more twisted than the human heart." Sometimes it is so hard for us even to think about the things of God.

But Jesus' Word to us is mercy. We can look at a crucifix and remember that He was forgiving us as He died. That is the wonder of the First Word, the miracle of forgiveness.

## Prayer

*Jesus, I love You. Let me stand close to Your cross, so close that I can hear Your dying Words.*

*Your Word of forgiveness, Lord, is very hard for me because it makes me face my own lack of forgiveness toward others. I am consoled with Your pardon, but have to struggle to imitate You. Help me to hear You in the deepest part of my heart. Give me the strength to accept the wisdom of this Word.*

*Bathe me in Your forgiveness, make me think of nothing else, let me make Your Words my own. Amen.*

# CHAPTER TWO

■■■■■ ■■■■ ■■ ■■ ■■■■■ ■ ■■■■■

# The Second Word

*Two other men, both criminals, were also led out with Him to be executed. When they came to the place called the Skull, there they crucified Him, along with the criminals — one on His right and the other on His left.*

*One of the criminals who hung there hurled insults at Him: "Aren't you the Christ? Save yourself and us!"*

*But the other criminal rebuked him. "Don't you fear God," he said, "since you are under the same sentence? We are punished justly, because we are getting what our deeds deserve. But this man has done nothing wrong."*

*Then he said, "Jesus, remember me when you come into your kingdom." Jesus answered him, "I tell you the truth, today you will be with me in paradise" (Lk 23:32-33, 39-43).*

One of my favorite characters in English Literature is Sidney Carton from Charles Dickens' novel of the French Revolution, *A Tale of Two Cities.* Carton was, says a dusty old *Encyclopedia Americana* given to the mission perhaps twenty-five years ago by a U.S. Navy captain in port, "a dissolute young English lawyer." He saves the aristocrat of conscience, the Frenchman Charles Darnay, from an English court, and later from the Jacobin guillotine, both times by taking his place, first figuratively and then literally.

The drama or melodrama of this character is that Dickens has a libertine-like Carton capable of pure self-sacrifice. He and Darnay are in love with the same woman, Lucie Manette, but Carton knows that she loves his rival more than him. Again in my old reference book, "He spontaneously resigns himself to acting only as her devoted friend, his unselfish love for her being his redeeming trait."

After a life of selfishness, Carton finishes gloriously. His last thought as he ascends the guillotine is one of the best known bits of Dickens: "It is a far, far better thing that I do, than I have ever done; it is a far, far, better rest, that I go to, than I have ever known." Beautiful words, for a beautiful ending: few twists of plot are as satisfying as last-minute redemption.

I think the same way about the Good Thief, to whom the Second Word of Jesus is addressed. Only St. Luke's Gospel tells us about him. All that we know of the thief from the Scriptures consists of these few lines. How little the Bible tells us about this man! Traditionally, he has been called the Good Thief, but even that is a hypothesis. The Greek word used is translated "malefactor" or "criminal."

Some scholars have examined the idea that the two crucified with Jesus were politically involved in some way. Perhaps they were fellow prisoners of Barabbas, the man released by Pilate instead of Jesus. Maybe they had even been involved with Barabbas in his "insurrection" against the Romans. We can only speculate on this matter, since Luke does not give us the details.

One hint about the crimes of the other men is provided by the Good Thief himself. He apparently considered his punishment just. *We are getting what our deeds deserve*, he says. Certainly the comment implies that the two criminals had taken lives themselves. If they were bandits, the murder of some of their victims would not have been a surprising occurrence. Even in our day, robbers often kill those they steal from.

Recently I was told of a band of almost thirty thieves who roamed about the area close to our mission in El Salvador. The group disbanded when the leader was captured, but their outlaw style was something out of the history books or legends of robber bands.

The poverty of the area, the loneliness of the roads and the topography, the availability of weapons, the short time elapsed since the war that had made everything uncertain — all of these made the conditions here for a lifestyle based on violence. Palestine in the time of Christ had similar conditions. The political situation made the instability even more favorable for armed bands. In my opinion, this is also the story of the criminals crucified with Jesus.

But there are criminals and there are criminals. Once I was celebrating a Mass in a medium security prison in Rhode Island and was impressed by a petition one of the men made. "Let us pray for the young people, so they don't make the same mistakes as we did and don't end up in this place," he said, in a voice barely under control. He was emotional thinking about his errors. I am sure that he too would have recognized in Jesus an innocent man, and would have been noble enough to defend Him.

Many commentaries have called attention to the confidence of the man in the mercy of Jesus. That confidence was one that presumed a degree of intimacy with the man Jesus that we do not see in others in the Gospel stories. He addresses the Lord by name. "Jesus," he says, "Remember me when you come into your kingdom." No one else in the Gospels addresses Jesus only by His name. From this intimacy legends have been made that the men had some previous experience. There is a legend that the Good Thief and Jesus had contact as children, in a desert inn where the Holy Family stopped one night on their flight into Egypt escaping Herod's persecution.

I am not sure that previous knowledge or contact is really a necessary hypothesis. Some men, even violent men, have a sincerity about them that enables them to establish rapport quickly. Their confidence in themselves is reflected in their acceptance of the truth. I knew a young Mexican man in the United States who had ended up on the wrong side of the law in several instances. He was a strong and a natural leader. Despite his troubles, I felt that I could trust him because I could tell that he would not lie to a priest. It is an interesting thing to reflect upon how the people's veracity does not always concord with their position in society. There are always some people, even some people involved in bad things, who are more truthful than others who have nice houses and good reputations.

In the story of the passion of Jesus, the Good Thief is a star of the truth. He corrects his fellow criminal for siding with the ugly crowd of detractors, and then directs some words to a wronged man. His respect for Jesus and for spiritual values can be assumed by the little he says. As in so many of the miracle stories, simple words indicate profound meaning.

The Good Thief is the last person to speak to Jesus. His were the only words of consolation and faith heard amid the shouts and the mockery. Jesus, who especially in the Gospel of St. Luke is the Savior of the outsiders, grants the outlaw a tremendous mercy. The Scripture scholar Father Raymond Brown wrote about this man, that although he only asks "to be remembered by Jesus, more is granted in terms of being *with* Jesus; for the response given by Jesus includes not only deliverance but intimacy."

The poor sinner, in his last words, makes an expression of faith both in Jesus' mercy and in His power. On a first-name basis with the Lord, the man sincerely seeks to make up for the mockery of the others. Respectful of the power of this holy man, he asks for His help. Faith is the courage and confidence to call on Jesus with assurance that He knows what is best for us.

What if we were present when Jesus had this dialog with the condemned man? I think that we would have to be moved by the presence of tenderness in the cruelest of contexts. Here are two men dying a horrible death, and both are moved to words of kindness and respect. The scene was macabre: an execution as public act and entertainment at the same time. The vengeance of the enemies of Jesus was combined with the vengeance of the State. It was not enough to see Him dead; they wanted to see Him dying.

But in that darkness, there was a ray of light which pierced the clouds: someone could come to love Jesus in the last hours of His life on earth. And Jesus loved him, and saved him. Few things are so moving as the kindness of the dying. Once a man I had just given last rites brushed my arm with his hand. "Do you need something?" I asked as I looked at him. "A mosquito," he said. He didn't want me to suffer the insect bite. No wonder Jesus says that those who give even a cup of cold water to His disciples will be rewarded. How important the intention is in all acts of kindness.

## Mary Magdalene

I can imagine Mary Magdalene watching the exchange between the three dying men on the crosses. The unrepentant criminal was no doubt filled with bitterness. It was a bitterness so profound that it made him take sides against the Innocent One. The angry crowd could have had no love for him. And yet, he had to know that his insult would make the enemies of Jesus happy. "Even this one knows," they would think, and laugh, "how ridiculous this man's pretensions were."

Mary Magdalene could have recognized the demon behind the attitude of the other criminal. "At least I am not as bad off as this one. At least I am not deluded like him." With the little breath he had, the man had to insult a fellow prisoner! How we need to feel superior to someone! We are suffering, but at least we are superior to someone else.

Assuming that the other criminal did not know Jesus truly was the Son of God, what did he achieve abusing this other condemned man? Could it have reduced his own physical torment? Would anyone hope to be pardoned at the last possible moment? What was the consolation that he sought? It was merely the illusion of superiority, the mirage which only cynicism offers us when we are in the pit of despair.

American English, at least, talks about, "taking it out on another." I think of the eyes of Mary Magdalene looking at this criminal who needed to feel superior to Jesus. While I am sure there would be sadness in those eyes, I think that there would be strength, too. Jesus had thrown out the demon of superiority with all the others. She had a heart that could be saddened but not embittered. That is perhaps why she ended up the first to know about the Resurrection.

I also think of Mary Magdalene being grateful for the gesture of the Good Thief. When we can't do anything for our friends, it means so much to us that others care about them. The Good Thief cared about Jesus. This was evident in the fact that he defends Him with what is practically his dying breath, and from what he says to Jesus. His presumed intimacy was joined to a delicacy of feeling. "You will come into your own, remember me," he was saying.

As in the case of Jesus saying, "Forgive them, Father," the words of the Good Thief are introduced by the imperfect tense, which literally means, "he was saying." This could indicate repetition, although not necessarily so. But it reminds me of the beauty of the words of the Good Thief as set to music by the brothers of Taizé (a Christian ecumenical group in France), which is also repeated like a mantra. The repetition emphasizes the emotional impact of the statement of faith. The Good Thief instinctively knew that all would pass but the love of Jesus. He was anticipating the kingdom as he asked to be included in it. Mary Magdalene must have appreciated such faith.

## The Beloved Disciple

We might suppose that there was a world of difference between the two men, the criminal and the young disciple. Nevertheless, the intense loyalty of the disciple must have been touched by the criminal's sincerity. I suppose that he could even have felt jealous of the Good Thief. After all, who wouldn't have wanted to end the day with Jesus in Paradise?

Cardinal Martini, in a reflection on the Gospel of St. Luke, has remarked on the tragic overtones of the exchange between Jesus and the Good Thief. The Lord came to save us all, but at the time of His death He could only count one who had achieved definitive salvation. Only the patience of God could support such a frustration. The universal will to save was able to free only a criminal, a violent man who, at the last moment, declared himself for Christ. Although he perhaps had heard of Jesus — of the miracles and the preaching — it would be impossible to presume that he had been somehow touched by Jesus' ministry.

The only one saved seems to have been saved by accident. He happened to be crucified next to Jesus. Many times in my priestly ministry I have had the experience that the persons to whom I have directed myself more self-consciously and from whom I expected more response have not responded as much as others whose reaction often surprised me. Surely, it would have been natural to suppose that the Incarnate God would receive more of a welcome from the priests of the Temple dedicated to His presence or from those, like the scribes and Pharisees, whose life was a constant study of His Word.

Instead, the people on the margin listened to Jesus. It was another sign of God's power working in and through weakness. Cardinal Ratzinger speaks of this in *Salt of the Earth*. He said: "The tenor of our faith is that God's distinctive greatness is revealed precisely in powerlessness. That, in the long run, the strength of history is precisely in those who *love*, which is to say, in a strength that, properly speaking, cannot be measured according to categories of power. So, in order to show who He is, God consciously revealed himself in the powerlessness of Nazareth and Golgotha."

The conversion of the Good Thief was a great lesson in salvation. When all looks lost, the grace of salvation appears. The fourth Gospel has a verse perhaps more famous than any other: "For God so loved the world that he gave his one and only Son that whoever believes in him shall not perish but have eternal life" (Jn 3:16). God had become man to save the likes of the Good Thief. The criminal would not perish because he believed in Jesus. We can imagine the Beloved Disciple taking the lesson in.

Another verse from the Gospel of John comes to mind. In Christ's priestly prayer for His disciples He says, "Now this is eternal life: that they may know you, the only true God, and Jesus Christ, whom you have sent" (Jn 17:3). The Good Thief was on the edge of eternal life. His salvation had been waiting for him, haunting His steps in good and evil until the very last words he would say. It is not a model we would suggest for finding God's grace, but it was a personal encounter with the saving, forgiving Jesus. He expressed his faith in Jesus, and that is how he came to know God's mercy.

"God is love" (1 Jn 4:16). This sentence is one of the most famous quotations from the writings of the Beloved Disciple. I imagine him seeing and hearing the exchange between two men about to die and recognizing the divine. Where charity and love prevail, there God is ever found. The story of the Second Word is about the charity of one dying man to another and must have touched the Beloved Disciple.

It is a priestly task to recover for God what has been lost to His grace. The Beloved Disciple saw Christ's priesthood acting in the rescue of this crucified sinner. The apostle witnessed the redemption of a soul, and his priestly heart must have rejoiced in the work of God's grace in the Good Thief.

How it should resonate with us, too, members of a priestly people. God's mercy at the last minute, a rough sincerity that wins forgiveness, two generous men dying next to each other: these elements are worth our contemplation. Trying to see the scene from the point of view of the disciple who wrote most about love can only help.

## The Blessed Mother

She had been told, of course, that He would cause the rise and fall of many in Israel, that He would be a sign of contradiction. Here was a case in point. Two men are crucified with Him; one curses Him and the other is saved.

What was she thinking during this exchange? The question is unanswerable with any certitude, because of the mystery every person is to another, and yet is worth considering because it makes us approach the reality of the cross. Standing with the Blessed Mother near to the cross puts us nearer to Jesus.

I think that she must have been relieved that in the desert of Calvary there would be this flower of faith. Someone else cared about Jesus, not just those who knew Him. And her mother's heart must have been open to the poor man. She could have thought of *his* mother, presumably absent. The sentiments of a mother, which sometimes seem so instinctive, are an instinctual grace, to say the least. God gives those who give life a certain tenderness, which can be denied and refused, unfortunately, but exists in some deep well of the soul.

The Blessed and Sorrowful Mother must have drawn from that well to feel compassion for the other. He was an honest man, although he had a bad past. Anyone close to Jesus must have felt some consolation in the words of the Good Thief. *He knows and has some feeling, this criminal who should know less than all these scribes!* That is what I imagine as the reaction of all three at the foot of the cross. The words of the guilty make great testimony for the innocent.

Beyond that, however, was the essential kindness of the Good Thief. His respect for Jesus while almost all the others were filled with disdain for her Son must have touched Mary deep in her heart. Intense situations can produce intense relationships. How many people, for instance, remember persons who helped them when they were in great difficulty, nurses who attended relatives or friends about to die, chaplains at hospitals, even lawyers or bank clerks, who, in a moment that was especially trying, offered unexpected sympathy?

I was called once to attend a dying woman and the experience was short but memorable. Only a few days earlier, and for reasons I do not understand, I had picked up a novel at a second-hand book sale which told the story of a young woman who had died of cancer. I don't usually look for this type of book, but I had seen the movie, and had been quite moved by it. My life very suddenly imitated art, for the woman I was called to confess was young, lucid, and surrounded by her young children. (I could not finish the book.)

The woman began making plans for her funeral right after her confession. *What had to be in order to arrange the Mass*, she asked. Then she wondered about our parish hall, and if we had caterers for a reception after the funeral Mass. She was in good spirits, despite everything, and so I dared joke at one point, "You know you can let us take care of some of this." She laughed, too, and so did those with her, although we all had just been in tears only moments before because of what one of her sons had said.

At her funeral, only three days later, I said that the experience of knowing her was like not going out until sunset on a beautiful day. You see the sunset, and think, "What a day I missed, but at least I can be grateful for this moment." Her friends and family were so grateful to me for the comparison; several of them mentioned it to me at the reception, which ended up being at a place much larger than the parish hall.

The family was so grateful to me for the hour or so I had spent at the bedside of the dying woman. Small kindnesses sometimes make for powerful memories and emotions. My father died of cancer at home after only a few months of diagnosis, an experience that was extremely intense for us. I still remember with great emotion how my brother-in-law Joe leaned over my father to kiss him and say, "We love you, Dad." I will be grateful to him for that for the rest of my life.

I really think that the Blessed Mother would have felt like that about the Good Thief. A small gesture can win our hearts at special times, and I am convinced this gesture would win the Immaculate Heart.

## Conclusion

Whether you identify with the last-minute faith of the Good Thief or with Jesus' compassion, there is great food for thought here. How do you hear this "Word"? Three very different men were hanging on crosses. Maybe we can identify with two of them. The Irish Nobel Prize winner for Literature, Samuel Becket, has a character comment in his famous play *Waiting for Godot*, "One of the thieves was saved. (Pause) It's a reasonable percentage." Does the "percentage" give you a good chance?

# Prayer

*Jesus on the cross, I love You.*

*As I stand near the cross, help me listen to Your Words with faith and love.*

*Let Your love for the Good Thief inspire and console me.*

*Give me some of that freedom to open myself to others, to never lose hope in them. Help me, Lord, to understand that You invite me, too, to paradise. Amen.*

# CHAPTER THREE

■■■■■ ■ ■■■ ■■■ ■■■■■■■■■■ ■■■■■■■

# The Third Word

*Near the cross of Jesus stood his mother, his mother's sister, Mary, the wife of Clopas, and Mary Magdalene. When Jesus saw his mother there, and the disciple whom he loved standing nearby, he said to his mother, "Dear woman, here is your son," and to the disciple, "Here is your mother." From that time on, this disciple took her into his home (Jn 19:25-27).*

The world has become an anthology of cultures. Computerization, special marketing, and the great resources at the disposal of the American civilization makes it possible for us to participate in other cultures and to be aware of them even across great distances of time and space. For example, I went to the art museum in my American hometown and got to see the Benin Bronzes, a collection of works of art from a civilization from the west of Africa from a time of the European Middle Ages.

Part of the exhibit included a description of the coronation of the king. What impressed me about the ceremony was what happened to the queen mother once her son was chosen as king. There were, perhaps, unhappy memories of matriarchy among the Benin, for the queen mother was forced to retire completely from the court. Although she was given a special place to live and was well cared for by servants, she was forbidden access to her son. In fact, she was never allowed to see the king again. She was a queen, but the basis of her status was a great renunciation. I suppose all this was to avoid influence, or mistaken policies, like that disclosed in the relationship between King Solomon and his mother Bathsheba in 1 Kings 2, when she becomes the inadvertent agent of her son's half-brother and rival, Adonias. Immediately afterwards, Bathsheba disappears from the Bible, like the mother of the king of the Benin from the reign of her son.

Scholars have always associated this Third Word of Jesus to His mother and His disciple to the only other scene in the Gospel of John where Mary appears, the wedding feast of Cana. St. John Chrysostom explicitly joined the two scenes in his commentary on the Gospel of John.

> [While the soldiers divide Jesus' garments] He Himself, though crucified, gave His Mother to His disciple's keeping, to instruct us to take every care of our parents, even to our last breath. When she came to Him at an inauspicious moment, He said: "What wouldst thou have me do, woman?" (Jn 2:4) and: "Who is my mother?" (Mt 12:48). But here He showed great tenderness, and gave her into the keeping of the disciple whom He loved.[3]

Most scholarship today finds much more to both scenes than a son's relationship to his mother. Instead of thinking that Mary had bad timing at Cana, and that Jesus was preoccupied for the physical care of His mother, Scripture scholars try to puzzle out the theological meaning of the two incidents. Mary is present at the beginning of the public ministry and at the end.

Both of her appearances in the Gospel are enigmatic, especially since Jesus addresses her both times merely as "woman." At Cana she provides the faith for the first miracle, seemingly even against the will of Jesus Himself, who talks about the fact that His hour had not yet come. The next time we see Mary in the Gospel of John is at the hour of Jesus' death, the hour the evangelist associates with the Lord's "glory."

All of this has a strong scent of mystery. Mary seems to disregard the Words of Jesus and then says what can be the rule of life of any good Christian: "Do whatever he tells you" (Jn 2:5). The same sort of mystery is obvious at the cross. The evangelist never says the name of Mary, and Jesus addresses her only as "woman." (The New International Version, presumably because of the use of the vocative case in the original, translates the greeting, "Dear woman," like something out of Shakespeare.)

There has to be more here than meets the ear. The radical German Bible critic Rudolf Bultmann saw in the scene at the foot of the cross the union of Jewish and Gentile Christianity. Most interpreters today do not agree with him, but do think that the revelation, "Behold your mother," has more to do with the life of the ordinary Christian than just an example of filial devotion.

The fact that this Word of Jesus about His mother is among the Seven Last Words should attract our attention. What Jesus said from the cross must have universal significance. Catholic tradition has always emphasized how the Beloved Disciple stands for the whole Church, which must take Mary "home." This taking Mary to our home means that the Christian life signifies identification with her. The Beloved Disciple from that hour (in Greek, what is translated as "time" is actually "hour"), took her into his home.

We need to place ourselves again on Calvary to understand the dramatic nature of this scene. Did the Roman soldiers see the holy man talk to His mother? Even if they could not understand the Words, I would think the sense of the communication would be felt. They had just divided His clothing among them. The spoils of execution could not have been too great, but John says that each of the four soldiers received a garment, and cast lots for the tunic that was woven in one piece. Did Mary take her eyes off her Son to look at the soldiers eager to steal the little He had left in the world?

The tunic for which the soldiers gambled has been the subject of some reflection and legend, famously in the Lloyd C. Douglas novel *The Robe*. There are those who say that the garment is an allusion to something the Jewish priests wore as described by the ancient Jewish historian Josephus. Others have thought that the fact that it was woven in one piece might mean that Mary herself had made it for Jesus. The fact that we read of the soldiers dividing up the garments just before Jesus talks to Mary and the Beloved Disciple perhaps explains that hypothesis.

Mary sees the soldiers rob Jesus of the clothes on His back. The poverty of Calvary is like the poverty of Bethlehem. Pope John Paul II, in his reflection on the way of the cross, said about the tenth station, where Jesus is stripped of His garments, that Mary could have thought, "This was the child I bathed." The marks of the scourging, the painful evidence of the fragility of the body, the complete defenselessness must have had an impact on the mother's heart.

I wrote a short story once in which I imagined the thoughts of a Roman soldier who remembered his mother at the time he saw Christ talking to His. Albert Camus, the great French writer, said what feelings a man had for fellow beings, he got from his mother. Were the soldiers so hardened by life that they were unmoved in the presence of the man's mother? The soldier in the story was moved.

Did the thieves on the crosses next to Jesus react? Did some of His enemies feel self-conscious when they recognized the mother of their enemy? Was Simon of Cyrene still there to watch? What would we have seen and felt there? Again we will have recourse to the three who listened.

## Mary Magdalene

Did Mary Magdalene think of her own mother as she heard Jesus speak from the cross? Did she have children of her own to think about? These are things to find out in heaven, but they direct our attention to how the saint could have heard the Words addressed to the other two witnesses at the foot of the cross.

Did she feel left out? The great director Franco Zeffcrelli seems to be aware of this possibility in his epic film *Jesus of Nazareth* because he invented a scene to link together the Blessed Virgin and Mary Magdalene at the foot of the cross. The centurion tries to stop Mary Magdalene from getting closer to the cross and implies that only family is allowed to approach. The Virgin tells the man that Mary Magdalene is family. Thus the scene places the mother of Jesus and Mary Magdalene at the foot of the cross together, something not clear from the synoptic gospels who have the latter at a distance.

John does not talk about the women who stand at a distance away from the cross, but makes a definite statement that the Virgin stands with her sister, also called Mary, Mary the wife of Cleophas, and Mary Magdalene. There has always been a great controversy about whether the Virgin had a sister by the same name, or if there is some mistake in the manuscripts. I have seen enough Hispanic families, who have a few Marías and Josés and distinguish them by their middle names, not to be concerned about the puzzle. What matters is the proximity to the cross, about which the Gospel of John is insistent.

Mary Magdalene is thus the witness of this Word in a special way. The other two at the foot of the cross, were also witnesses, but also directly addressed by Jesus. Did Mary Magdalene feel excluded? I suppose that would be a common reaction in our time, when we are so full of ourselves that we resent it when access to practically anything is denied. A saint, however, is free of such pettiness. A saint loves with disinterest, a word even the meaning of which becomes more elusive for us each day. Disinterested means without a personal agenda, free from any conflict of interest.

That is how I see Mary Magdalene in the moment she heard this Word. The demon of selfishness, which controls so much of our emotional life, had been thrown out of her by Christ. Tradition has depicted Mary Magdalene as an ascetic saint. I remember seeing a bronze of her in Florence by one of the great masters in which she looks almost like John the Baptist, her long hair covering a body through which every bone seems palpable. Her asceticism is a sign of victory over self. She was free of what enslaves many of us.

Our culture is not very open to the negation of self. Often, almost reflexively, we use pseudo-scientific terms or pop jargon to defend ourselves from thinking about self-denial. It is sickness, a poor self-image, or a false understanding of what God wants —we say — which leads us to subordinate our desires and feelings to something other than ourselves. Commentators have talked about the philosophic narcissism of the age. Even the altruism of our sad times needs to be served up as self-fulfillment.

The hard law of the spiritual life is that it requires a victory over self. St. Ignatius of Loyola wrote out his spiritual exercises to enable the disciple to "conquer" self. If this sounds foreign to us, it is perhaps because we have grown up indulging ourselves. Only concentration on the other can free us from making ourselves the center of the universe.

I knew a priest who was invited to celebrate Mass at one of Mother Teresa's convents in Rome. Mother Teresa was present, and the priest told the sisters that they represented Christ for him and were an inspiration. Afterwards Mother Teresa spoke to the priest.

"Never tell the sisters they are Christ," she told him. "They are to see Christ in the poor they serve." The priest was shocked at the harshness of this, and repeated the story to many. What he didn't seam to appreciate was that even the most charitable work can be infected by self and selfish concerns. Often liberation has to take a violent form so that freedom can be won, like in the life of nations. Thank God, however, that, unlike in the life of nations, the only victim of the violence is self-interest.

Most religions point to a liberation of self in some way. Buddha denies the whole world in order to deny the self. Islam preaches submission to the will of God. Jesus taught the way of the cross, "If a man will come after me, let him deny himself and take up his cross, and follow me" (Mt 16:24 KJV).

That liberation of the soul should be reflected in our emotional life. I write this way without pretending to have achieved what I describe. But the ideal of selflessness is too important to be discounted because of our petty failures. I have been reminded lately, by means of a new spiritual director, how lax I have become about seeking the Lord. This new director emphasizes that he who does not advance goes backwards, that the spiritual life is always a climb on a slippery slope. Since this priest is from another culture, he has helped me realize how much our American culture, with its Gospel of self-fulfillment, can make discipleship very difficult.

Mary Magdalene is a symbol of the spiritual life because she was set free by Christ. I think of her listening to Jesus speak to His mother and His disciple with complete freedom of mind, heart, and soul. She did not have to say, as some of us might, "And what about me?" She was free to appreciate the love that was communicated in this Word. She could rejoice in true charity, like the love of which St. Paul wrote in 1 Corinthians 13.

Her freedom would enable her to understand the mystical importance of the human love of a son for His mother who was made infinite by the Incarnation. The healing and the purification of all human relationships, which is part of the salvation promised by Christ, is seen first of all in the relationship of Mary with Jesus. She is "blessed among women" because, as Elizabeth says, "blessed is she who has believed . . ." (Lk 1:45).

It was the privilege of Mary Magdalene to be present for this Word, and her silent witness should inspire us. I suppose the lesson of Mary Magdalene in this Word is for me whether I can be free of myself enough to rejoice in the love of others. Mary Magdalene, whom I think of as rejoicing in the love of Jesus and Mary and the Beloved Disciple, is an example for me. How good it would be to stand near to that love and to be content in silence.

## The Beloved Disciple

How many times had Jesus directed His Words to the Beloved Disciple? At the Last Supper, when Jesus says that one of the twelve apostles will betray Him, Peter gives the Beloved Disciple the signal to ask the identity of the traitor. This simple signal tells a great deal about the relationship of Jesus and the Beloved Disciple and Peter. The theologian Hans Urs von Baltasar has many beautiful pages about the three in his book of reflection on the papacy.

There are several constellations of three in the Gospels. Peter, James, and John are seen several times in special relationship to Christ, including the Transfiguration and the Agony in the Garden.

Scholars debate whether John the son of Zebedee is the same as the Beloved Disciple and Evangelist, but that is not the point here. What is of interest is seeing Jesus in the emotional context of some special relationships. Lazarus, Martha, and Mary are another set of persons related in a special way to Jesus, both individually and collectively.

Sometimes the triad includes Jesus himself. Peter, the Beloved Disciple, and Jesus are another triad. Jesus, Mary, and the Beloved Disciple represent another constellation of persons united in grace and love. These relationships must have a deep mystical significance for us. We need to see them as an invitation to the interior life of Jesus.

The Beloved Disciple takes his new mother to his home, "from that hour." Obviously this sounds like a note preserved by the people who knew the Beloved Disciple, the community who knew that there was always this relationship with the Mother of Christ as part of the reality of their discipleship. We do not need to know the specific thoughts of the disciple when he heard this Word because we know the result of his hearing.

There is a model here of all discipleship. Instead of an exchange of words, there is silent acceptance of the Word and His will. There is obedience and love. When we act out the Stations of the Cross at our mission here in El Salvador, we have the Beloved Disciple put his arm around the shoulders of Mary to indicate his acceptance of the responsibility of caring for the mother of the Lord. The few Words of Jesus speak a whole world of relationship, "Here is your mother, here is your son," hide within themselves commitment and feeling and integration of life. He does not say, "Treat this woman as if she were your mother." Rather he indicates what is really a change in the Beloved Disciple's personal history. Now this woman is a part of his life. She is involved in his personal identity. She is his mother.

This change is not just a responsibility or a task. It is a gift of relationship: she will be a mother to him. This privilege is so great that it is no wonder that this Third Word has always been interpreted in its broadest possible application. This cannot be a merely personal note. This last testament has to be directed to all of us.

Blessed Josémaria Escrivá de Balaguer, the founder of Opus Dei, was a man of profound Marian inspiration. He said of the Sorrowful Mother that if we looked into her heart we would see she has two children, "Jesus and you." This seeing ourselves in the Beloved Disciple was an important part of the Blessed Escrivá's spirituality, and points to how you and I can assimilate the mystery of this Word.

If we stand with John we realize both the care Jesus has for us as well as our responsibility toward others. We can see both vocation and response here. Neither is a question of "Jesus and me." Always there is the reality of relationship in grace. The Holy Trinity is the model of the life of grace for precisely the reason that the relationship of the three persons in God is always open and not self-enclosed. The deepest mysteries of our faith are the Trinity and the Incarnation. Both have to do with a love without boundaries. The mysterious boundlessness of God's love, however, has an anchor in flesh, a concrete focus, which is the man Jesus. Because of the Incarnation, we know that all grace is relationship, because it comes to us through one Mediator.

And that Mediator was the loyal Son of a human mother. Some of the most beautiful passages about the love of God are found in the writings of the Beloved Disciple, the Gospel of John and the epistles. I think that it is possible to understand that there would be some reflection in these passages of the love that the Beloved Disciple had experienced in his own life. That love, if we take this Word of Christ from the cross seriously, had a Marian element.

Much of what I know of love and self-sacrifice I learned from my mother. I am sure that one of the ways that the disciple learned about love was from the heart of the woman who was both his mother and the mother of his Lord.

The Church asks of priests a special devotion to the Mother of God. This is found in both the code of canon law and in the Second Vatican Council document on the priesthood. A priest should be able to identify to some extent psychologically with Christ in whose person he acts sacramentally. Of course this applies to relationship to Mary, also.

Recently, I came across an interesting example of an application of both the priest's identification with Christ and thoughts about his mother. Blessed Josémaria Escrivá in a retreat for priests once gave a profoundly ironic but interesting reading about the priest's relationship with his own mother and the comparison with Christ and Mary. Considering the example of Calvary, he said, it would be much better if a priest's mother survived her son, as Mary did Jesus. He said this even as his mother lay gravely ill, and, in fact, his mother died before the retreat was completed. I find this story very moving because it indicates the love that Blessed Josémaria had for his mother and reflects the sentiments of many priests. It also shows how disappointing life can be, "sometimes," said Dickens, "to the hopes that do our nature its highest honor."

As a priest, I could not read the story about Blessed Josémaria's mother without thinking about my own case. Obviously, I, too, would prefer that I would go ahead of my mother to heaven. I am afraid that sounds strange, but I know that my grief for my mother would be a burden nearly impossible for me to bear. And if I died before my siblings, I would have the confidence of knowing that they will always take care of my mother.

These unusual and a bit unwelcome thoughts, "If I would die before my mother," and "If I could express my desire that she be well cared for" help me to appreciate the tremendous grace that the Beloved Disciple received. Jesus was expressing faith in him. He trusted him with the person with whom His human life was most identified. Even in the pain of the moment, this grace must have consoled the Beloved Disciple.

Consoled, and perhaps challenged him, also. I was told by a dying woman once to try to look after her son. He was in the throes of painful adolescence and had taken her terminal illness very poorly. As it turns out, the young man was never really ready to talk to me, and now is a few thousand miles away. I pray for him, remembering his mother's recommendation, but I wish that I could do more.

This Word, for us, however, has become pure consolation. We do not have to worry about the Blessed Mother, nor see her life end on earth. We have only to welcome her and accept her protection and grace. The Beloved Disciple's responsibility has become the blessing of all disciples. His was the work, but ours is the grace. That should makes us grateful to stand next to Him in prayer.

### The Blessed Mother

Did she remember the first Word addressed to her in the Annunciation? Did she think of the praise of Elizabeth, who saw her as the luckiest of mothers? Did she recall the wonder of the shepherds and the grave homage of the wise men? How could she not remember the words of Simeon as she watched them crucify her Son? A sword would pierce her heart, the old holy man had said. Would it be possible at this terrible moment to forget the child lost in Jerusalem? Did she say to herself, "And so this was His father's business"?

The life that started with the Annunciation was ending. More than ever, she would be alone in the sense that so much of her experience was incommunicable. St. Luke's Gospel emphasizes this when he mentions twice that the Virgin "kept all these things in her heart." With whom could she share it? The Virgin is key to the ministry of Jesus, although she seems to have had little to do with it. Nevertheless her role is recognized in the Gospels of Luke and John in quite different ways — the Annunciation/Infancy Narratives of St. Luke and the "mother" (her name is never used in John) of the wedding feast of Cana and the foot of the cross in St. John. Mary had given birth to the Word, but added few words herself. Her mission, connected to the secret life of Christ in Nazareth, was a hidden one. Her appearance on Calvary and in the event of Pentecost therefore have so much more significance.

Her silence was unbroken from Cana to Calvary and beyond. Her selflessness meant renunciation, even of her access to her Son, as we can see in the synoptic gospels when Jesus is teaching and is told His mother is waiting outside. Although she did not say, "He must increase and I decrease," like John the Baptist, she evidently retired to a silent discipleship. At Calvary, we can presume, she was still doing what she did all of Jesus' life: "Keeping these things in her heart." In this dramatic scene when she returns to view, we have to wonder what kept her heart from breaking.

The fact that her Son took such pains to include her in His community was a sign to her as well as to the community. It must have been a consolation, especially considering the way that Mary had to share Jesus with others during His whole ministry. And His consolation was not just pity for her, but feeling for His disciple. "Please be a mother to him," is another way we can look at this Word. Jesus was sharing His concern for His Beloved Disciple with His mother.

There has been a good deal of controversy in recent years about whether the pope should officially declare the Blessed Virgin "Co-Redemptrix." A pontifical commission recommended against a solemn declaration, and some bishops and scholars have thought that more time is needed for the acceptance of this truth and the refining of its definition.

I confess that I am a bit deaf to the difficulties of the definition. St. Paul indicates that Jesus makes room for all of us in the work of redemption when he says that his personal suffering makes up for "what is still lacking in regard to Christ's afflictions" (Col 1:24). This means that Christ gives all of us the opportunity to participate in the work of Christ's redemption. Certainly in this work, Mary's participation excels all others. That is what any sort of definition will clarify and help us to understand. All of us co-redeemers with Christ is the vision that is implied in our recognition of Mary as co-redeemer *par excellence*.

For centuries, the Church has recognized that Mary is the New Eve, the first who has received the grace of Christ's redemption. Christ is the New Adam, the symbol of redeemed humanity because He is *redeeming* humanity. Many scholars have seen that John, who has Jesus say "woman," when He addresses His mother, is echoing the creation narrative which says, "she shall be called 'woman' " (Gen 2:23). Mary the New Eve, created for and by the Son of God, thus becomes a new "mother of all the living." This view of Mary is really the same as the title Co-Redemptrix.

Obviously, this recognition will add nothing to the grace God gave the Blessed Virgin. Human recognition cannot add to divine favor. It only helps those who recognize give glory to God. The recognition of Mary's instrumentality is a celebration of how she learned to serve. The English poet Kipling has a character in one of his stories say to another, "You haf too much Ego in your Cosmos." That is certainly true of me, and perhaps of all of us. There is too much "self" in our universe. This was not true of Mary. Her focus was always beyond herself.

The French poet Alfred de Musset said, "Nothing makes us as

great as a great sorrow." This, like so much that is said by poets, needs some restriction, for there are those who are not ennobled by suffering. Rather, they are embittered by it. Mary's freedom from self, however, shines through in her suffering with Christ. The identification of Mary with Jesus, her standing by Jesus silently, her reflection in her own heart of God's mysterious will for her, are all examples of nobility in suffering. Her great sorrow really was a sign of greatness.

In her own way, in the way of a mother, Mary made up for what was lacking in the suffering of Christ. That is what this Word helps us to see. Her special role in salvation stands out at the foot of the cross. The compassionate thoughts of Jesus for Mary should be enough to make us love her as our mother. The fact that He cared so much for her should make us care for her. How much we need to take her into our homes and our lives.

## Conclusion

My own experience of Christianity has never been separated from Mary. It is hard for me to imagine how a person can be close to Jesus and not feel a mystical love for His mother. That was how I was raised, although I know that I am lucky to feel this way. There are Catholics who do not feel natural about Marian devotion. After a trip to the Holy Land, I received a letter from a fellow pilgrim who said she was jealous of the way I talked about Mary. She wished that she could have such a feeling of friendship for Mary.

Even now, as I sit at my desk here in El Salvador, I pray for that woman. God will bless her honest search for grace, I am sure. My thoughts also turn to you who are reading this. "Whoever you are holding this in hand," to quote Walt Whitman, I hope that you, too, can listen to this Word of Jesus with a heart open to Mary.

It seems to me that Jesus is clearly indicating here that every disciple has to make room for her. Even if a traditional Catholic Marian piety might not seem possible to you, you still need her in your discipleship. The Marian message of John's Gospel can be seen in two key phrases. She says, "Do whatever He tells you." And He says, "Behold your mother." This seems important for every Christian.

The same Kipling I quoted earlier has a poem about Mary that I find very interesting, since the poet was not a Catholic. It is called "Prayer for the Dying."

> O Mary, pierced with sorrow,
> Remember, teach and save
> The soul that goes tomorrow
> Before the God that gave;
> As each was born of woman,
> For each, in utter need,
> True comrade and brave foreman,
> Madonna, intercede.
> Amen.

Mary as comrade and foreman? There is a Mary for everyone, as a priest said in the missionary preparation center I attended when he heard that the Blessed Virgin had been made a general in the Bolivian army at some point. What is interesting is that Kipling joins together the "each was born of woman," with categories usually associated in masculine milieu, "comrade" and "foreman." Nevertheless, Mary as companion for the journey of life and guide in its work are not ideas that are difficult to accept.

The most popular prayer to Mary asks for her intercession "at the hour of our death." This has to have something to do with the fact that she was with her Son as He was dying. His Word to her and to the Church as He died should remind us of the confidence ex-

72

pressed in the words of the Hail Mary. How many times we say prayers and do not think of their implications. "Now and at the hour of our death," obviously should remind us of Him at whose hour of death she must have been praying, too. We are revisiting that hour in this meditation.

The Beloved Disciple did not mention the earthquake in Jerusalem at the hour of the Lord's death, nor the strange occurrence of the Temple veil rent in two. He leaves out the prayer for pardon and the exchange with the Good Thief. But it was not possible for him to leave out Jesus' thought about His mother and His disciple. What a lesson there is for us in that.

## Prayer

*Jesus on the cross, I love You.*

*Thank You for the privilege of hearing this Word.*

*You invite me to share the love of Your mother and Your disciple, all that You had left on earth.*

*Give me that same generosity of spirit, and let me treasure Your mother as my own, with all of Your disciples. Amen.*

# CHAPTER FOUR

■■■■■■■■■■■■■■■■■■■■■■■■■

# The Fourth Word

*At the sixth hour darkness came over the whole land until the ninth hour. And at the ninth hour Jesus cried out in a loud voice, "Eloi, Eloi, lama sabachthani?" — which means, "My God, my God, why have you forsaken me?"*

*When some of those standing near heard this, they said, "Listen, he is calling Elijah."*

*One man ran, filled a sponge with wine vinegar, put it on a stick, and offered it to Jesus to drink. "Now leave him alone. Let's see if Elijah comes to take him down," he said (Mk 15:33-36).*

The Gospels are sometimes extremely ironic, but perhaps nowhere like this scene of the only Word of the Seven Last Words reported by Matthew and Mark. The "Teacher" gives His last lesson from the cross. He quotes a psalm in Aramaic. Those listening do not catch the reference to the psalm. They assume that He is calling Elijah, and someone is then moved to give Jesus a bitter wine to drink.

What could be more symbolic of the apparent failure of Jesus? The last lesson of the Master is lost on the people who hear it, because they hear Him wrong. St. Matthew and St. Mark report only this Word of the Seven. And so in their Gospels there is this overwhelming irony: even His Last Words were misunderstood. He recites a psalm, which expresses confidence in God despite the attacks of enemies, and they think it is a desperate call for help.

This fits with the dynamics of Mark's view of discipleship as a series of frustrated lessons which point to the mystery of death and resurrection but which are not understood until after everything has been accomplished. The first one who seems to "get it" is the Roman centurion who says, "Surely this man was the Son of God!"(Mk 15:39b). The irony of this insight is that the man is a pagan and has participated only in the last hours of Jesus' life.

Even though Mark says that Jesus was calling out in a loud voice, the people heard something else. This is another example of the misunderstanding and misinterpretation that dog Jesus' steps in the Gospel. But why Elijah? Obviously, part of the reason is the first two words in the original. The Greek cites the Aramaic, transliterated, but does not tell us that El and Elohim were names of God. Thus it is possible to hear "God" but think "Elijah." It is interesting that both Mark and Matthew assume this information is irrelevant.

But there is a reason why the crowd thought that Jesus was calling on Elijah that goes beyond the similarity of the pronunciation of the words. At the time, Judaism had already developed a special place for Elijah both with regards to the Messiah and to the individual believer. The prophet Malachi predicted that Elijah would come back before the Messiah and be His herald. But contemporary Judaism at the time of Jesus had an even more personal belief about the prophet who was so powerful and who, mysteriously, had been carried to heaven in a fiery chariot — he came to the aid of the sick and dying.

The gesture of the man who gave Jesus the bitter wine to drink was not necessarily a mockery. Some scholars see in this scurrying for wine some other impulse. Did the man believe that Elijah came to the dying like some kind of angel of mercy? Did Jesus' cry of the heart touch him in some way, and make him want to do something to alleviate the crucified's pain? The fact that the wine was mixed with vinegar makes us think that this was added mockery, and his "let's see if Elijah comes for him," sounds like skepticism, but there is nevertheless a possibility that the man was well-intentioned. People have done many nonsensical things with good intentions.

For me, the ambiguous involvement of the man in the passion of Christ can be taken symbolically. You could be that close to the dying Jesus, and yet not understand. This reminds me that we can all be witnesses in some way of the mystery of Jesus' self-sacrifice, and still "not get it." There can even be moments in which we think, "Now let's see whether Elijah comes to take him down." We don't always believe in His power.

St. Mark shows a Jesus who is surrounded by enemies. There is no Good Thief in this Gospel (in fact both thieves seem to mock the Lord, according to his recounting); the women supporters look on from a distance; the chief priests have come out to jeer at Jesus; the atmosphere is absolutely antagonistic.

That is why the psalm Jesus quotes is so appropriate. Psalm 22 is the prayer of someone who feels ambushed and alone. The prayer to God is so desperate because the enemies are so cruel:

> But I am a worm, and not a man, scorned by men
> and despised by the people. / All who see me mock
> at me; they hurl insults, shaking their heads: / "He
> trusts in the LORD; let the LORD rescue him. / Let
> him deliver him, since he delights in him" (Ps
> 22:6-8).

The enemies of Jesus are saying and doing the same kind of things. This makes even more ironic the citation of the psalm. They do not understand that Jesus is comparing His experience to the psalmist's. The prayer is about their cruelty, and they do not understand it.

In the psalm, the enemies are not only cruel, but also terrifying. They are like wild bulls, like "roaring lions tearing their prey," like a pack of wild dogs. All of these images are of terror; there is something inhuman about the enemies, something as fierce and frightening as wild predators.

The reaction of the psalmist, which sounds very much like the experience of dying, is probably a description of the human sensation of fear. The overall feeling of weakness, the heart melting within, and the mouth incapable of speech are all sensations that accompany fear.

> I am poured out like water, all my bones are out of joint. / My heart has turned to wax; it has melted away within me. / My strength is dried up like a potsherd, and my tongue sticks to the roof of my mouth; / you lay me in the dust of death (Ps 22:14-16).

In the Agony in the Garden, Mark tells us about Jesus' fear. He took Peter, James, and John along with him, and He began to be deeply distressed and troubled. "My soul is overwhelmed with sorrow to the point of death," He said to them. "Stay here and keep watch" (Mk 14:33-34).

This is the moment remembered in Luke as that in which the Lord sweated blood because of His anguish. Jesus was not immune to the human experience of fear, that is clear from Matthew, Mark, and Luke, all of whom wanted to emphasize the suffering humanity of Jesus. The author of the letter to the Hebrews also remembered this Jesus who struggled.

> During the days of Jesus' life on earth, he offered up prayers and petitions with loud cries and tears to the one who could save him from death, and he was heard because of his reverent submission (Heb 5:7).

Once when I was discussing the passion of Christ in a Bible study, I noticed that some people were uncomfortable with a Jesus who was so obviously shaken before the crucifixion, and reluctant to meditate on the force of the prayer, "My God, my God, why have you forsaken me?" But one woman said, "I am glad to know that He was afraid, too, and that He felt abandoned. I can relate to that feeling."

The vulnerability of Christ is the story of our salvation. Had He not suffered, we would not be free. His humanity was the instrument of God to save us. This is the mystery of the Incarnation. God made Himself powerless in order to rescue us. He could feel pain, He could bleed, and He could die.

He could even feel alienation. That is for me the most important insight of this Word. Jesus felt the alienation of sin to the point that He felt forsaken by God. Even though the psalm has to be taken as a prayer and, taken as a whole, as an affirmation of faith in God, it is obviously a description of the feelings of a man who experiences forsakenness. This abandonment includes the sentiment of estrangement, which some philosophers have called alienation. Alienation is the intense feeling of what Chesterton called "the secret treason of the universe." When we say we feel "out of sorts," we mean that nothing seems really to work the way it is supposed to, as if we were at odds with life itself.

Alienation has been the subject of much of modern literature. The German writer Franz Kafka captured the anguish of modern man in an absurd universe. His *Trial* has a character identified only as Joseph K. who finds out that he is in a judicial proceeding but is never told his crime. Life becomes an official sort of conspiracy, and, at the end of the novel, Joseph K. is condemned without ever knowing what he is accused of. The absurdity portrayed in the novel is that there is guilt without knowledge and a sense that life is an inevitable and losing battle.

The same feelings are present in many forms of mental illness, but there is an uncanny grain of truth even in schizophrenia, as anyone who has had to deal with its victims knows. Life itself, in the sense of the business of living, seems sometimes a process of estrangement for many of us. Doubts and a feeling of forsakenness leave us saying, "My God, my God, why have you forsaken me?" even when we do not give voice to that terrible thought.

This Word of Jesus names what is sometimes unnameable for us. The absolute vulnerability expressed ought to be a consolation for those of us who have passed through dark valleys of despair. While it can be that you have never felt yourself pressed to that extreme, I doubt that you do not know and perhaps love someone who did feel that estrangement. The forsakenness of Jesus is a great symbol of solidarity for all of us.

Our meditation on the alienation of Christ should serve us well not only in understanding our own feelings of depression and despair, but also and especially, the feelings of others ambushed by a sense of abandonment in the midst of hostility. The Christ who says this Word from the cross speaks to the heart of the problem of existence: how are we to maintain faith in a cruel and disappointing world.

Taking the perspective of the three witnesses at the foot of the cross, we can analyze and understand the depth of meaning of this prayer on the lips of Jesus in the very hour of His sacrifice. For each witness, I imagine a different aspect of the alienation of the cross. The purpose of the exercise is to enter somehow the complex reality of the cross, which contains much more than any one of us could discover.

## Mary Magdalene

What did she think of this prayer of Jesus expressing His feelings of abandonment? Since I think that she was someone who had personal experience of alienation, I imagine that the Words entered into her soul. What saint could not feel the depths of the love of Christ expressed in His willingness to suffer even this abandonment? A saint who had been liberated from seven demons had to know something about estrangement and feelings of abandonment.

Within that reality of forsakenness, the abandonment of others would be a demon with which St. Mary Magdalene would be familiar. That demon haunts us all. When a child wakes up alone, sometimes he cries like a lost soul. The instinct of survival in a child demands closeness to the mother.

Recently a mother left her little girl just for a moment to go to confession outside of one of our country chapels, where the confessional is a spot under the trees, and the girl screamed and cried until her grandmother let her come close to her mother. I saw the panic in the little girl's face, and her tears. I thought: this is an example of the fear of abandonment which exists in every human heart. Adults also have this fear, although perhaps not so near the surface. How many people stay in hurting and unhealthy relationships because they cannot bear to be alone? How many people can never be alone in the house without some noise, the television or the radio to keep them company? There is a feeling of panic in being alone.

Christ on the cross was alone in a way that He had never been before. Emotional rejection means loneliness and pain, the pain of

the heart for which there is no medicine. Part of the drama of crucifixion was the great deal of emotional rejection that it included. I
think that the presence of Judas Iscariot at the Last Supper was the
beginning of the passion. Christ's reference to the betrayal in the
context of the last meal He shared with His closest followers reveals
His human consciousness of the plot against Him. What human heart
would not be troubled by the fact that a close friend had joined forces
with enemies? I wonder what hurt more, the betrayal or the hypo-
critical kiss that was its sign.

After the arrest, the experience of Jesus was of disrespect and
rejection. He is slapped by the temple guard when He speaks with the
high priest. He is taken before Pilate, who shows his anti-Jewish preju-
dice in his conversation with Jesus. "Am I a Jew?" asks Pilate, and the
question reveals a world of information about what the relationship
between Jew and Roman really meant. Jesus, victim of the Jewish
religious establishment, was also a victim of Roman anti-Semitism.

The rejection continues when Pilate proposes that the crowd
choose between Jesus and Barabbas. Who of us has not been
wounded by the rejection of others implied in choices? Sometimes
people remember even trivial rejections, like those of boys picking
teams on playgrounds. Could Jesus' human heart not have felt the
wound of the ridiculous contest proposed by Pilate? Barabbas means
in Aramaic, "son of the father." Who would want to be put in the
position of competing with another for a chance to live? One "Son"
of the Father had to die, but the experience of that sea of hatred
which is implied in the cry of the crowd to free Barabbas had to be
a part of the suffering of Christ.

Weak Pilate continued to seek some way to avoid the crucifixion. His pathetic subterfuge of scourging Christ seems to have been
so that the sight of the suffering of the prophet would move the
people who hated Jesus to soften at "the man" whose weakness they

beheld. With the scourging, which was a punishment sometimes fatal for the weak, there was the sideshow of the Romans who mock the "King" of the Jews, another way that Jesus was a victim of imperial anti-Semitism.

The Roman soldiers, who were probably always aware of the fanatic Jewish nationalism directed against them, delighted in this weak Jew who was presented to them as a king. The spitting, the slapping, the cruel crowning with thorns had to be emotionally painful. Physical humiliation is psychic pain, and Jesus was subjected to the humiliation of public mockery in the nakedness of the cross, where the parchment proclaimed to all who could read, "Jesus of Nazareth, King of the Jews." How many times we look at a crucifix and do not remember that the letters INRI were a last insult? The dividing of the clothing between the four soldiers who crucified Jesus was also a last injury. Before death could take Him, the little He had was divided in spoils.

To the bitter end, He was mocked and subjected to what would be called today psychological torture. Even if Mary Magdalene was not aware of all the details of His humiliation, she must have had enough knowledge to feel the terrible force of the hatred of Jesus' enemies for Him.

An older priest, a cousin of my grandfather, once was entering a rally against abortion in an auditorium in Cleveland. Some pro-abortion activists stationed themselves at the door as a kind of emotional gauntlet, screaming their selfish slogans. One of these pro-abortionists saw my cousin's clerical collar and spit in his face. It still shocks me to think of it, but he said to me, "Richard, it is all right. They did the same to Jesus."

Sympathy and identification with a person includes feeling the emotional hurt of another. Melville wrote in *Bartleby the Scrivener*, "To a sensitive being, pity is not seldom pain." Mary Magdalene probably had suffered her own share of rejection in her life. Now she stood watching as waves of hatred and rejection broke over the head crowned with thorns. She suffered seeing the mystery of evil in human hatred directed at the One whom she loved and who had rescued her from alienation.

How frightening it is to know the evil that lurks in the hearts of men. The testimony of the first American soldiers who came upon the evidence of the Holocaust was of pained shock. It evokes the construction of the poet E.E.Cummings, "manunkind." The horror of knowing that people can be so unfeeling strikes to the soul. Sometimes I think the paralysis of some of those opposed to abortion is due to the difficulty of responding to the enormity of hatred and evil of present-day life. If not for faith, one might despair.

Imagine being a witness of the crucifixion. I can only try to understand the depth of the pain that a disciple of Jesus would feel standing at the foot of the cross and seeing that, until the bitter end, His enemies only wanted to see Him suffer more. Reflecting on Mary Magdalene, we can approach that mystery of evil and stare at it, like someone looking down from a perilous cliff, with one person between you and the edge. In the history of the tortuous human heart, the crucifixion must be the worst example of human perversity: the Son of God comes to save us and we nail Him to the cross.

Jesus had referred to this hatred which surrounded Him in John 15:18-25, "If the world hates you, keep in mind that it hated me first. . . . But now they have seen these miracles, and yet they have hated both me and my Father. But this is to fulfill what is written in their Law: 'They hated me without reason.' "

But all is not despair. Mary Magdalene, who witnessed some of that fierce hatred against Jesus, and who had to suffer very much doing so, was also the first to witness the Resurrection of Jesus. Her witness to this Word must take that into account. God the Father did not abandon His Son. The tremendous irony of the Gospels presumes that we will appreciate that fact. The alienation of Christ was something He freely assumed.

For that reason, there is a tremendous hopefulness even in thinking of Jesus' emotional suffering. Obviously, Jesus was free of the many complications and neuroses which afflict modern North Americans. But His heart was like ours and it could feel what we feel. That thought ought to be a liberation for us.

The Ancient Greeks saw in dramatic art a movement of the soul that they called *catharsis*. The meaning of this word has occupied volumes of scholarship but basically has to do with an emotional response of identification with the sorrow or struggle of another that takes a person beyond himself or herself to a new understanding. What is lacking in many movies and books today is true catharsis, a resolution that takes us further than the characters, which may not be the famous "happy ending" which some seek, but which brings one closer to the truth.

The story of Mary Magdalene can provide a catharsis for the Christian who reads it well. We can move with her from despair to seasoned hope. She is, the Church says, "the Apostle of the Apostles," the first to bear the good news of Jesus' Resurrection. But she stood in the shadows of that despair before she could be the bearer of hope. And so it can be for us, also. If we can imaginatively stand in the shadows of the cross, we will be able to meet depression and emotional alienation. Like Mary Magdalene, we may require a further revelation, but just being there will have helped us.

## The Beloved Disciple

The Beloved Disciple was an eyewitness of the crucifixion of Jesus. Although this might make one expect the most graphic portrayal of the suffering involved, John's Gospel is very sparing on the description of the suffering of Jesus. There is no attention to the Agony in the Garden, for instance. He does, however, include one note not mentioned by the other Gospel writers: the breaking of the legs of the two thieves on either side of the Lord. This practice, called *crurifragium*, was used to hasten the death of the crucified. The Beloved Disciple reports that when the soldiers came to Jesus, they did not break His legs. The Gospel of John sees in this a sign with theological meaning.

That theological meaning had to do with a great theme of Christ's sacrifice, which is a theme in all of the writings of the Beloved Disciple. The Lord Jesus was the Lamb of God, the victim whose sacrifice was salvation. Exodus had ordered about the Passover lamb, "Do not break any of the bones" (Ex 12:46). The Beloved Disciple had seen the sacrifice of the Passover lambs in the temple, when they must have been slaughtered by the hundreds. Had this disciple been sent to the Temple for the last Passover Jesus celebrated with His apostles?

The question is interesting because of the insistence on the image of the Lamb of God in what are called the Johannine writings. The Book of Revelation refers to Jesus as the sacrificed lamb thirty times. I think that intensity might have come from seeing the actual sacrifice on the cross, including the opening of Jesus' side by the thrust of the lance. This flesh that hung upon the cross was given to us as food, as the sixth chapter of John emphasizes. This crucified one was the one to be enthroned in heaven, like the Lamb of God in the fifth chapter of Revelation.

The contrast between the glory and the gore is one of the remarkable things about the lamb, "looking as if it had been slain" (Rev 5:6). My own reflection on the Beloved Disciple's possible reaction to this Word of Jesus — "My God, my God, why have you abandoned me?" — is to follow through the image of the sacrifice.

The violence of the sacrifice is thus sublimated to the spiritual reality of Jesus' self-giving.

Pain is a kind of physical alienation. The body that experiences pain is alienated from itself. People who have cancer or heart problems or paralysis feel the contrast between their own wills and the resistance of the body. Something is part of them but not part of them. The poet Auden captured some of this tension, writing of the death of William Butler Yeats:

> But for him it was his last afternoon as himself,
> An afternoon of nurses and rumours;
> The provinces of his body revolted,
> The squares of his mind were empty,
> Silence invaded the suburbs,
> The current of his feeling failed:
> he became his admirers.[4]

As I wrote this chapter, I was engaged in something like a death-watch. My Uncle John was dying of cancer and was no longer conscious. The provinces of his lungs and his stomach had revolted against him and he could not eat or breathe normally. The contrast between his person (he was a man, like Yorick, of "infinite jest") and his poor body declining to death was a portrait of physical alienation. We were counting the seconds between his breaths and trying to separate our memories of him from the ruins of his body.

The inspiration of the writer of the Gospel of John was to see in the death of Jesus its spiritual and life-giving essence. The blood and water that flowed from the side of Christ after his death gives us a striking image of life from what is dead. It also shows us the priestly sensibility of the Beloved Disciple who was able to spiritualize what had to be a human trauma, seeing the death of the One he loved more than anyone or anything. This represents a kind of transcendence of alienation, a seeing beyond it to a whole new reality.

The abandonment or forsakenness had to reach this point. The alienation of pain had to work its absolute result. He had to die. Only in death was Jesus to set us free to live. The physical death of Jesus was the beginning of new life, which would have for nourishment the blood and water coming from the side of the Savior. The sacrifice of the Lamb became sanctification. The despair of death was only of the birth pangs of the new reality of grace.

The Beloved Disciple recounted how Jesus said that the disciples might feel sad at His death, but should think of the sadness or physical distress of a woman in labor. This image has come to my mind because my mother commented on my uncle's dying in a similar way. She said, "Waiting for someone to die is like waiting for a child to be born. Sometimes it seems that it is very close, but we cannot know exactly, we have to wait." Is that how the Beloved Disciple learned to see the hour of the cross? "So with you: Now is your time of grief, but I will see you again and you will rejoice, and no one will take away your joy" (Jn 16:22).

Of all those on Calvary that day, the Beloved Disciple was the most likely to hear and understand the prayer of Jesus which is this Fourth Word. He would be the most likely to understand the Jesus was praying a psalm. However, his Gospel does not make reference to it. The Gospels always represent a selection — the fourth Gospel even says that if all that Jesus did would be written down it could not fit in all the books on the planet. Still, it is a curious omission, unless the Beloved Disciple just assumed that we would be acquainted with the other Gospels.

And there is another possibility. Jesus was praying the whole time on the cross. We know the Last Word of the Seven is a citation of a psalm, also. Perhaps the Seven Last Words represent only the key elements. Many people under stress concentrate on prayer, even though that concentration sometimes suffers. I remember trying to pray the Rosary once during a guerrilla attack on the town I lived in. I know someone listening to me would say I only stammered "Hail Mary," and "Holy Mary Mother of God," because my nervousness made me mix them up.

The Beloved Disciple could have seen Jesus at prayer on the cross and said "Behold the Lamb of God," the words he told us the Baptist said of the Lord. Certainly the sacrifice of the cross made an indelible impression upon him. He could see beyond the poor wasted body of Jesus to the enthronement of the Lamb in Revelation.

We should follow the lead of the Beloved Disciple and see the hour of death as also the hour of glory. This is true not only of Jesus, but also of every Christian. In one of the most common of our prayers, we anticipate the "hour of our death." If we can have the insight to see in that hour the commencement of our glory, we will have gained a great deal. I think of this as I remember my poor uncle fighting for breath, thinner than I had ever seen him, reduced practically to a physical minimum that made his tumors palpable, almost visible.

If we could see death as the completion of our sacrifice we would pass beyond the alienation to which our flesh is heir and know true peace. I think we can stand next to the Beloved Disciple and look together at the physical alienation present in human life: disabilities, pain, sickness, and death itself. Sensing the disciples solidarity and love, we will be strengthened.

## The Blessed Virgin Mary

There was another type of alienation present on Calvary. It was not physical or emotional, but spiritual. This was a kind of alienation that we must strain to understand because we are much too familiar with it. We live this alienation because we live in an environment of sin and failure to cooperate with God's grace. We have never known a complete freedom from the effects of sin, because sin has cast its shadows onto our very souls, as the Church's doctrine of Original Sin teaches us.

The abandonment that Christ felt on the cross was especially spiritual. St. Paul says that Jesus, who did not know sin, was made "to be sin for us" (2 Cor 5:21) The forsakenness of Jesus was that becoming sin to save us. He took upon Himself all our sins. Colossians 2:14 says, "having canceled the written code, with its regulations, that was against and that stood opposed to us, he took it away, nailing it to the cross." The body of Jesus was nailed to the cross, which means that it contained in some way all the guilt of humanity.

When, in the Agony in the Garden, Christ sweats blood and wonders if it is possible that the cup pass by Him, it was this alienation which He wanted to avoid. It was a spiritual eclipse felt within His own body, this being made sin for us. To take out all the poison in the environment, He had to breathe it all in. The toxicity of sin was concentrated in the passion and death. That is why many imagine that the cross was so heavy. Its spiritual burden, or rather its anti-spiritual burden, was enormous. The acceptance of Jesus of the bitter cup of suffering was the acceptance of mystical joining of all the poison of human evil and its history of failure, selfishness, and cruelty.

Mary would be sensitive to this spiritual poison like no one else. Her Immaculate Heart must have understood the real drama of the abandonment suffered by Jesus on the cross. He had to let the darkness fill Him in order to win victory over it. This was the only way for us to be saved, but I think we do not understand the mystery of evil that it meant receiving. It was as if one person would ask to receive the virus of a plague hoping that he would produce antibodies that would save others.

John Henry Newman has an insight that I find very thought-provoking. His ethical ideas have a good proportion of aesthetic principles, like the poet Keats who said, "Beauty is truth, truth beauty." Newman described the operations of conscience as essentially emotional in application. In *The Grammar of Assent*, he wrote this about conscience:

> Conscience too, considered as a moral sense, an intellectual sentiment, is a sense of admiration and disgust, of approbation and blame: but it is something more than a moral sense; it is always, what the sense of the beautiful is in certain cases; it is always emotional . . . [C]onscience excites all these painful emotions, confusion, foreboding, self-condemnation; and on the other hand it sheds upon us a deep peace, a sense of security, a resignation, and a hope, which there is no sensible, no earthly object to elicit. "The wicked flees, when no one pursueth"; then why does he flee? Whence his terror? Who is it that he sees in solitude, in darkness, in the hidden chambers of his heart?

Cardinal Newman has a meditation on the Agony in the Garden in which he describes the painful process by which Christ assimilates all the guilt of human evil. Newman's aesthetic inclination is expressed when he tells us of the awful ugliness of sin and its terrors for Jesus, who was completely pure. In a creative meditation, Newman imagines that Jesus would have the feelings associated with all the guilt of all of humanity. That spiritual-emotional burden of ugliness is so terrible that it causes Jesus to sweat blood. The spiritual abandonment produced by the ugliness of sin that He bears in himself begins at the Agony of the Garden. This adds a mystical dimension to all the suffering of the passion, because besides the visible mistreatment, there is an invisible sense of alienation that Christ carries with the cross.

I was once called upon to go to court with a mother of a migrant worker who was involved in an awful rape case. Because the mother was so afraid of what would happen to her son, she asked me to translate the testimony being heard. It was a bit of a confusing case because of the woman in question, but the details of what had happened, from both points of view, were nauseating. My face was red, and I stopped translating at a certain point, although the woman kept asking me, "What are they saying?"

A sense of shame had come over me, and I felt terrible even though I was not guilty. I suffered the embarrassment of the woman, the situation, and the fact that whatever had happened was disgustingly inhuman. What would my feelings have been if the guilt of the deed had been imputed to me personally? Jesus bore our guilt and the alienation from God that it caused on Good Friday. Part of the supernatural pain He felt was the awareness of all the selfishness and cruelty of humanity concentrated in a time period of less than twenty-four hours. The mystical agony of Christ was imperceptible to all the others, but I think not to Mary. She felt the shame imposed upon her Son like a suffocating weight.

The German theologian Hans Urs von Balthasar once mentioned that Christ had submitted Himself to the "humiliation in the baptism of sinners in the Jordan." The phrase made me think of something I had not thought of before. Jesus began His public ministry taking upon Himself human sinfulness by submitting to the baptism of John. Some medieval theologians thought that John the Baptist was born without Original Sin. He had been conceived with it, but the movement of the Holy Spirit that happened when Mary visited Elizabeth indicated his freedom from the sin.

However it is formulated, certainly John the Baptist was especially sensitive to sin. That explains his reaction to the Pharisees who wanted baptism, and, of course, it makes understandable his initial refusal to baptize Jesus. What sins were there to wash away? It was truly a humiliation for Christ to line up with the sinners at the Jordan, a humiliation that prefigured that of the cross. No wonder Jesus had to force John to baptize Him.

An even stronger experience of the injustice and the paradoxical cruelty of Jesus bearing the guilt of all of humanity could be felt by Mary at the foot of the cross. Mary would sense both the humiliation and the guilt of sin that Jesus had decided to carry, not so much in the cross as in His own person. No soul could have understood the torment of Jesus more than Mary. Free from sin, she could sense all the evil that invaded Jesus so that He could put it to death with Him on the cross. All the power of the concentration of human betrayals through all of history would die with Him on the cross.

When Jesus said, "My God, my God, why have you forsaken me?" Mary might not have recognized the reference to the psalm, as no doubt the Beloved Disciple did. But she would have understood the abandonment in its most terrible form. The severest test of the human will of Jesus was the one that asked Him to drink in all the poison of sin, to take on alienation from God and to embrace forsakenness. The greatest sorrow of Mary must have been to see this moment, although one of her greatest consolations must have been to know the love with which Jesus abandoned Himself to His mission.

Standing with Mary at the foot of the cross, we should ask God for more awareness of the ugliness of sin and the separation from grace, which is its result. The saint who said she would rather die than commit a venial sin knew about the alienation from God that is the root of every sin. This is a knowledge that comes with holiness, and is denied to most of us, but it is something to strive for and, in fact, beg of God. Perhaps you could take a moment to reflect on the alienation of sin as you have experienced it in your life. Mary can help you to see both how much we need to free ourselves of it and to focus on Jesus who has defeated that alienation by the cross.

## Conclusion

"This is for all the lonely people," begins a popular song of a few years ago. My own meditation on this Word of Jesus is that it is for all of us who have felt forsaken. The meditation took me through various aspects of alienation. We are not always aware of the alienation with which we live every day. It is something we have a steady diet of — on the news, in the Church — and it is lurking very near our own sense of self. Alienation is part of the ambience of our lives, but it is masked frequently by other distractions. There is alienation in our relationships. There is alienation sometimes in our relationship with our own bodies because of pain, sickness, and psychological traumas. Finally, there is alienation in the life of our own souls. This Word of Jesus speaks to all of that. The abandonment expressed by Jesus is a bridge for all us. He connected himself to our feelings of abandonment and alienation. Our forsakenness is taken up in His.

This Word is for all the forsaken people . . . He was there. He knows.

## Prayer

*Jesus on the cross, I love You.*

*This prayer of Yours comes from a suffering heart. Let the weakness You suffer in this moment be my only strength. Give me honesty in prayer and resignation to the Father's will. Help me always to remember that You have been in the shadow of despair.*

*Let this Word pierce my heart and purify my spirit. Amen.*

# CHAPTER FIVE

# The Fifth Word

*Later, knowing that all was now completed, and so that the Scripture would be fulfilled, Jesus said, "I am thirsty." A jar of wine vinegar was there, so they soaked a sponge in it, put the sponge on a stalk of the hyssop plant, and lifted it up to Jesus' lips ( Jn 19:28-29).*

There is an old song sung in the Good Friday processions in El Salvador about this scene. It surprised me as I walked in the procession of the Holy Burial because it connects the idea of the vinegar with the death of Jesus almost exactly as St. John's Gospel does. The Spanish is very simple, as is the verse structure.

> Tomando el vinagre
> Y mirando a su madre,
> Su espíritu se entregó.

The rough translation is:

> Drinking the vinegar,
> And looking at his mother,
> He gave up his spirit.

All of the Gospel writers thought this detail important. John apparently relates it to the prophecy of Psalm 69, verse 21: "They put gall in my food and gave me vinegar for my thirst." This is obviously meant to be a suffering, and many commentaries have seen the gesture of offering the wine-vinegar to Jesus as a kind of final insult. The great St. John Chrysostom, the patriarch of Constantinople, said this about it:

> Now, please notice the callousness of the bystanders. For, even if we have innumerable enemies and have suffered irremediable harm from them, on seeing them dying we take pity on them. However, these men were not even then softened toward Him, and did not become more kindly because of what they saw, But rather more savage, and increased their mockery. Offering Him a sponge soaked in wine, they gave Him a drink in the way in which they offered it to condemned criminals, since it was for this reason hyssop was employed in addition to the sponge.[5]

This reading of the incident, however, is not the only one. In fact, there are various differences among the Gospel narratives about this sponge on the hyssop. Both St. Matthew and St. Mark say that one of the bystanders offers the vinegar. However, Matthew seems to imply that the others at the cross criticize the man for doing so, because their response to the gesture is, "Now leave him alone." Mark, on the other hand, has the man himself saying, "Now leave him alone." St. Luke does not agree with the others that it is a bystander who offers the wine, and says that the soldiers were the ones who did it.

St. John, in this and so many respects, is unique in that he is the only evangelist who records that Jesus said, "I thirst." This makes possible a compassionate motive for the gesture. He is thirsty; only this cheap wine is available. All of these details and differences can give us an idea why some people dedicate their lives to Bible interpretations. There seem to be a variety of interpretations about the offering of the vinegar.

However, perhaps the meaning we are looking for has more to do with memories of Jesus' thirst than the motivation of those who offer the cheap wine. The fact that the Lord's last drink on earth was vinegar is almost too perfectly symbolic of the suffering and disappointment that dogged His steps here. This is given more significance if we look at other passages where Jesus talked about thirst in a symbolic sense. Jesus' Words at Jacob's well to the Samaritan woman about the satisfaction of thirst are also to the point here. There is also the beatitude, "Blessed are they who hunger and thirst for justice."

There is also the image of drinking that Jesus used to indicate commitment. When His disciples ask to sit at His right and left in heaven, He asks them whether they can drink from the same chalice as He. At the Last Supper, He told His disciples, "For I tell you I will not drink again of the fruit of the vine until the kingdom of God comes" (Lk 22:18). In the Agony in the Garden, Jesus asked that He not have to drink from the cup prepared for Him, but says, "not my will but thine be done." In the garden, when Peter apparently wants to resist Jesus' arrest with arms and cuts the ear of the high priest's servant, the Lord says, "Shall I not drink the cup the Father has given me?" (Jn 18:11). When the soldiers offer the wine in Luke, they mock Jesus as a "king," which is ironic since they witness the start of the realization of the kingdom in the atonement of the cross.

All of this indicates that this thirst of Jesus can have great symbolic meaning. We need to meditate a bit about it.

## Mary Magdalene

She knew something of thirst. Not just in the physical sense of the body's desire for liquids, but in the symbolic sense of the sensation of need. Thirst indicates what is lacking to us, our dependence on what is outside of us and the inevitability of appetite. All seven of her demons must have known this, but one most especially was preoccupied with her feeling unsatisfied. For that demon, Mary Magdalene's thirst for meaning had to be constantly misdirected toward what was never going to satiate her.

For ages, Mary Magdalene has been the symbol of what the American poet Delmore Schwarz called "the scrimmage of appetite everywhere." These words are the last line of his poem entitled "The Heavy Bear." It is an interesting depiction of St. Paul's insight about how the flesh contrasts with the spirit. The poet imagines his carnal self as a heavy bear which follows him around shadowing his actions and even interfering with his relationships. Part of the third stanza reads:

> That inescapable animal walks with me,
> Has followed me since the black womb held,
> Moves where I move, distorting my gesture,
> A caricature, a swollen shadow,
> A stupid clown of the spirit's motive,
> Perplexes and affronts with his own darkness,
> The secret life of belly and bone.[6]

The description of our appetite as a heavy shadow distorting all our movements is apt, and can bring to mind people we know who have not been able to put order in their lives. Many people are desirous of precisely what is dangerous or even always harmful to them. On some busy street corners of San Salvador, there are young men who beg money by playing with torches. They swig kerosene and spout flames while traffic is stopped at the light. Then they extend their hands and walk between the cars collecting the equivalent of quarters from the captive audience. Most of these men appear to be glue-sniffers, and you can look at them and count their ribs, their young bodies are so ravaged by their habits. For me, they are an example of how desire makes so many of us play with danger. Their sense of their insufficiency did not lead them to spiritual things but to pure escapism, the soothing nihilism of dulled consciousness.

They are not alone. All sorts of people have allowed a thirst for pleasure to become an addiction. The contortions of relationships, the destruction of families, violence in all of its multiple forms, all of these flow from the restlessness of desire. "The nature of desire is to be infinite," said Aristotle, and those who desire the wrong things sometimes appear to be caught in an infinity of traps. It is always good to remember that some very great saints were like that before their conversion. There is a Spanish saying, "Great sinners make great saints." We would all do well to remember St. Augustine's famous, "There but for the grace of God go I," when we see a person ruined by desire.

Mary Magdalene had almost been ruined by it. The saint is practically the icon of the war between the flesh and the spirit. The great medieval book of saints, *The Golden Legend* by Jacobus de Voragine, claims to discern some of this from the saint's name:

> Mary is called Magdalene, which means "remaining guilty," or it means armed, or unconquered, or magnificent. These meanings point to the sort of woman she was before, at the time of, and after her conversion. Before her conversion, she remained in guilt, burdened with the debt of eternal

punishment. In her conversion she was armed and rendered unconquerable by the armor of penance: she armed herself the best possible way — with all the weapons of penance — because for every pleasure she had enjoyed she found a way of immolating herself. After her conversion she was magnificent in the superabundance of grace, because where trespass abounded, grace was superabundant.[7]

What is important here is to understand that desire cannot merely be but transformed. In the calculus of penance, every pleasure was replaced with sacrifice. The love of Christ permitted a kind of transfiguration of appetite and sensuality. In the case of St. Mary Magdalene the great ascetic, this has meant the love of God as a consuming fire.

What did she think of Jesus' thirst? Did she associate it with her own sense of insufficiency? It would not have been such a step to see His thirst symbolic of His whole life and frustrated ministry. He had wanted something more. He had been thirsty to accomplish what God wanted of Him. He had been given vinegar to drink.

Perhaps Mary Magdalene had heard of the story of Jesus with the Samaritan woman. There, at Jacob's well, Jesus had been thirsty, too (as well as tired). But his thirst had inspired a thirst in the woman, when He tells her, "Whoever drinks this water will be thirsty again, but whoever drinks the water I give him will never thirst" (Jn 4:13). She apparently does not believe Him at first, for she is very sarcastic, "Sir, give me this water so that I won't get thirsty and have to keep coming here to draw water."

I think that Mary Magdalene could have sympathized and even identified with the woman at the well. She, too, had been thirsty before she met the Lord. She, too, had been rescued. She, too, would encounter the Lord unexpectedly on Easter, a meeting much more enigmatic than that of the Samaritan. She, too, would become a messenger. The Samaritan went to her town with the news of the prophet, which resulted in the conversion of the whole community. Mary Magdalene went to the community of the disciples with the news of the Resurrection. There is even a further parallel in that the belief of the townspeople of Samaria and the apostles in the end is based upon direct experience of the Lord.

The story of the Samaritan woman reveals the appropriateness of a symbolic interpretation of Jesus' thirst. One passage helps make understandable the other. The first thirst brought about the conversion of the woman and eventually of the whole village. St. Augustine, in his commentary on Job, said about Jesus at the well, "He who asked for a drink had thirst for the faith of the woman." The second thirst was a kind of ultimate message of Jesus' desire for souls.

I do not think that Mary Magdalene was necessarily aware of the message of Christ's thirst as she stood at the foot of the cross. Probably, it was just another evidence of the cruelty and injustice of the cross for her, another reason to feel for Jesus. When we see a dying patient in pain, how it pains us! Besides all this, He feels thirst, too, she might have thought.

Afterwards, when she had seen Him risen, she would understand. She could feel then the symbolic force of this thirst. She could understand that He had thirsted for us. Armed with our knowledge, we can stand beside Mary Magdalene in the dark hour of the cross and never lose hope, because we know about Christ's victory over death. We should not forget, however, how Jesus' thirst for us continues.

# The Beloved Disciple

He was the evangelist who said that the Word had become flesh and dwelt among humankind. He said in his first epistle that he proclaimed what "we have heard, which we have seen with our own eyes, which we have looked at and our hands have touched" (1 Jn 1:1). The tremendous truth of the Incarnation, of God become man, necessarily shapes all that we think about, but especially how we see other human beings. Hans Urs von Balthasar said that the fact that one particular hand was divine makes each time we shake hands a possible encounter with God.

This truth is certainly behind another citation from St. John, "For anyone who does not love his brother, whom he has seen, cannot love God, whom he has not seen" (1 Jn 4:20). The parable of the sheep and goats in Matthew 25 has the same point. Who can forget, in regard to this Word, which Jesus said of the just, "I was thirsty, and you gave me to drink"?

The American writer J. D. Salinger had a series of stories about the Glass family, a Jewish-Catholic tribe from Manhattan famous for their appearances on a radio quiz show. In the novella *Franny and Zooey*, Salinger has Franny recall for Zooey how the children were told to give their best performance for the people listening in. They were to shine their shoes, which of course would not be noticed on the airwaves, for "the fat lady," an imaginary member of the audience who was seen as especially needy. The children were to do their best for the fat lady, who is Jesus in another guise. In this case, it was "I was lonely and depressed, and you comforted me." Salinger was merely repeating the old lesson that the other is Christ, especially when the other is needy.

This was no doubt behind the reason that a modern-day saint had such devotion to this Word of Jesus. Mother Teresa of Calcutta ordered "I thirst" to be written above the cross in all the chapels of the houses of the Missionaries of Charity, the communities of brothers and nuns that she founded. I came to know this because of my friendship with some brother Missionaries of Charity in El Salvador who had a nursing home for poor men in a city called Mexicanos, part of the great urban sprawl that is San Salvador. Mother Teresa came to El Salvador, and visited their house.

She did not entirely like what she saw. Instead of the traditional crucifix and the words "I thirst" over them, the brothers had commissioned a local man to paint a modern kind of Calvary on the wall. I had admired the painting, which, although primitive in style, showed a great deal of raw talent for drawing (something which abounds in El Salvador). The scene was a bit political, however, and the brother superior had almost apologized for it the first time I saw their chapel. It included details of the state of war in El Salvador, like helicopters and scenes of violence by the military.

I was at the house when Mother Teresa visited. We had an open air Mass for the barrio celebrated by the auxiliary bishop of San Salvador, at which Mother Teresa spoke a few words. There was a crush of people at the Mass and in the house and I had no time to talk to my friend the superior. He told me to call him soon, and, when we got together, he told me about Mother Teresa's reaction to the chapel.

"This is very good, but not for the chapel, not for praying," she had said. She wanted the traditional crucifix and the "I thirst." The superior didn't think twice. When he showed me the chapel the next time I was there, the mural had been painted over. The standard format of the Missionaries of Charity had replaced it, with the Word of Christ in homemade calligraphy on a piece of white paper cut like a scroll. I cannot think of this Word without recalling my reaction when I entered the re-decorated chapel.

Mother Teresa wanted the brothers to concentrate on Jesus' thirst.

For her, the essence was that Jesus was the one who thirsted ("it is I who thirsts") and so every other distraction had to be suppressed. The hidden mural for me was a story about how we have to put aside our own agendas in order to focus on the Lord. Blessed Josémaria Escrivá de Balaguer said about similar situations: "What is offered to God in incense is not wasted."

We all know about Mother Teresa's work with the dying. I can easily imagine her holding a dying man in her arms and giving him something to quench his lips. I think of an uncle of mine who received nourishment only by a feeding tube in his abdomen for years after an accident destroyed his brain. The nurses or my aunt used to wet a sponge with water just to quench his sense of thirst. It was obvious how much he needed to assuage that sense of dryness.

That image of my uncle comes to my mind thinking about the moral meaning of this Word because it makes me see how he was made like Christ in that most terrible of circumstances. Helpless, unable even to say that he was thirsty, my uncle was like the Lord on Calvary. That thought does not make it easier to remember the seven long years in which my uncle was frozen in a last look of farewell, but it gives meaning to his suffering, and to ours with him.

If we can see Christ in others who suffer, we have the essential element of Christian morality. Jesus thirsty on the cross is a sign that all those who are in need bear his image. The disciple who loved Him knew this well. John's profound understanding of the Incarnation might not have started on Calvary, but certainly had to include this suffering. John, who has a serene Christ in his account of the passion (in contrast to Matthew, Mark, and Luke), needed to include this note of vulnerability. To stand with John on Calvary, we have to see Jesus in flesh and blood. And then we can realize that reflections and reminders of Him are all around us.

# The Blessed Virgin Mary

The first thirst He experienced was for the milk of her breast. Thirst, like all physical discomfort or pain, is a sign of danger for the body. The body risks dehydration just from ordinary functions, like respiration. The fluids that make up the complex organism that is our body require constant replenishment. By some delicate system, the brain is alerted of the liquid composition of the body and orders us to find water. The baby feels thirst.

The organic machinery of life is a wonder even as we see greater and greater human ability to work on its mechanics. It is even more wonderful when we consider that divinity has submitted to humanity's limitations. Psalm 50 seems ironic in this connection. The Lord says in verse 12, "If I were hungry, I would not tell you, for the world is mine, and all that is in it." Nevertheless, when He was thirsty, He decided to say so.

Mary was intimately aware of that thirst when she was a nursing mother. It was part of the rhythm of her life. Part of the vulnerability of God expressed in the Incarnation was the fact that God became so dependent. The woman who blessed the breasts that nursed Jesus could not have known the metaphysical implications. In Jesus we meet a God who was hungry and thirsty, a God who had to be rocked to sleep, a God who accepted the material straitjacket that is the flesh. The Word became Flesh and became needy.

This is a thought that can scandalize us. That is perhaps why this Word from the cross is so important. This God thirsts. He has desire for something beyond Himself. This could almost be a definition of humanity. We are creatures not sufficient to ourselves. This is the widest possible interpretation of the word "thirst." Part of the tremendous sacrifice of the Incarnation of Jesus' embrace of our vulnerability and neediness, even of our emotional neediness.

I remember very well when I first heard this thought articulated. My pastor when I was a seminarian was a tough ex-Navy chaplain who also was something of an intellectual. In fact, he was more involved in ideas than most of my seminary professors were. He subscribed to the French Dominican theological journal called *La Revue Thomiste*. I remember quite well his excitement one day when he told me that he had just read, in French, an article about the Sacred Heart of Jesus that had made him think a great deal.

The French priest had written that one of the consequences of the Incarnation was that divinity loved us with a human heart. This meant for him that there was a divine expectation of a response from us. Every human relationship included an element of waiting for a response from the other. No human act is completely disinterested in that the human heart gives itself when it loves. Human love, even divine-human love like the love of the Sacred Heart, always involves some kind of connection. That connection would seem impossible to think of in a God who was based upon pure philosophy. A God who has a beating heart, a God familiar with the heart's fragility, with tears and disappointment, could only be revealed to us personally; it could not be a deduction from some abstract principles.

A God who thirsts is the old scandal of the cross: a God who reveals Himself as vulnerable. The vulnerability means He suffers for us, He thirsts for us. Jesus is not "co-dependent" or as emotionally weak as some of us, but nevertheless He experiences the human desire for a response. Even the heart of Jesus, understood as the seat of affections, can be disappointed and can suffer from our lack of response.

His thirst had to have some impact on Mary. She must have suffered His thirst, too, because of her identification with Him, and because of a mother's natural solicitude. How frustrating to see Him this way! I can imagine Mary thinking something like, "As He entered this world He leaves it, but now I cannot help Him."

She had been there when He first experienced thirst in the stable at Bethlehem. She had probably taught Him the words "I thirst." She had seen Him thirsty many times in His life: because of the hot sun in the summer, because of the games He played with companions as a child, because of His sweating in the hard physical work of carpentry in an age before motors. I wonder if she saw this thirst as part of the string of thirsts in his life.

Did she associate it with the psalms that talk about the thirst for God? Psalm 63 has a verse which is very appropriate for meditation with respect to Calvary.

> O God, you are my God, earnestly I seek you; /
> my soul thirsts for you, my body longs for you, in
> a dry and weary land where there is no water
> (Ps 63:1).

The dryness of life points to glory because it is an indication that what we have here is not the whole story. The soul thirsts for God and that is why Jesus, who is our Savior and our model, also thirsted. All the images of grace which use water in the Bible, memories of the desert and reflections of the aridity even of the cultivated parts of Palestine are echoed and synthesized in Jesus' thirst on Calvary. On the lips of Jesus it becomes a kind of ultimate religious imagery.

We need God. This life does not satisfy us. We are always going to be thirsty, like Jesus on the cross, until we are with Him in glory. I am not saying that the Blessed Virgin would have articulated the meaning in this way, but I think that she would have responded to its meaning. Even as she wished that she could give Jesus something for His thirst, even as she suffered with Him, even as her tears were the only water in sight, she could have seen that "I thirst" is like an ultimate verdict on the world.

He was not satisfied. How can we be? Obviously spiritual people need to be at peace and even happy. But not satisfied. Our hearts are restless until they rest in the Lord, St. Augustine taught us. Meditating with Mary on this Word we can think of how she could have echoed Jesus' Word. She, too, thirsted for something better. She, too, knew the radical insufficiency of this world. She, too, thirsted for the end of injustice just like any number of mothers who see their sons die by violence every day in this world of ours.

It should remind us to be thirsty, too.

## Conclusion

There are three types of non-literal senses of Scripture, says the *Catechism of the Catholic Church* — the symbolic, the moral, and the one in terms of the hope of future glory. The three witnesses in this Word seem to take us in the three different directions.

The symbolic interpretation should have us thinking about Jesus' desire for us, how much he loves us, and his anxiety to save us. The moral interpretation should make us recognize Christ very close to us, still saying, "I am thirsty." The interpretation in terms of the future glory should make us think that this world can never satisfy us without making us less spiritual. For each of these points, it is well worth the time we spend with the three at the foot of the cross.

## Prayer

*Jesus on the cross, I love You.*

*Help me with this Word of weakness and suffering so that I may better understand Your love for me and the love I should have for my brothers and sisters.*

*Give me the grace to meditate on this Word and to enter into its mystery.*

*Let me never forget Your thirst. Let me help You in Your thirst and let me thirst with You and for You. Amen.*

# CHAPTER SIX

■■■■■ ■ ■■■■■■ ■■■■■■■■■ ■■■■■■

# The Sixth Word

*When he had received the drink, Jesus said "It is finished" (Jn 19:30).*

The Greek word *tetelestai,* which is translated here as "It is finished," could also be translated, "It has been accomplished." All translation is at least partly interpretation, and many scholars have talked about how the word *tetelestai* can have many nuances. I think that the meaning of accomplishment is an important note here, because it gives a sense of completion and fulfillment. It is not just an ending, but the way it was intended to end.

It is also, of course, terribly ironic. He drains the cup of suffering to the end, and then says, "Mission accomplished." To whom was this addressed? Certainly the bystanders would be surprised at the notion that the crucifixion represented things going according to plan. Only much later would it become clear to the disciples that the Messiah had to suffer and die, and they would remember how Jesus had tried to prepare them. In the Resurrection appearance on the road to Emmaus, Jesus says to them, "How foolish you are, and how slow of heart to believe all that the prophets have spoken! Did not the Christ have to suffer these things and then enter his glory?" ( Lk 24:25-26).

It certainly looked like a total defeat. King Francis I of France wrote after the battle of Pavia, "We have lost all but our honor." The followers of Jesus might not have been able even to say that much. St. Peter had shamed himself, the other apostles were afraid, and the only male follower with any courage was the Beloved Disciple. The women disciples, who had more valor, were able to witness the fact that Jesus had died a humiliating death, in the company of criminals, the object of tremendous hatred. And yet He died announcing that He had fulfilled what He had come to accomplish. This would be almost harder to accept than the acknowledgement of defeat.

We have a different perspective, of course, but we are not necessarily better placed to understand the meaning of this Word. Who can understand why Christ had to suffer? It is as hard to do as it is to understand injustice. There is a tremendous temptation to bitterness when faith meets evil that does not even bother to disguise itself. If you have ever witnessed an abuse of human rights and felt powerless against it, then you know some of the bitterness of this Word of fulfillment.

In the village where I live, I recently went to the wake of a man killed by robbers. The thieves had ignored the pleas of the wife and children of the victim and shot the man in cold blood. The helplessness I felt praying over such a casket is part of the ugly power of evil in this world. That helplessness must have been felt by the three witnesses, also. Jesus was a victim of injustice, of hatred and violence, and was yet able to say: "It is accomplished." What did they think about it?

We should remember that this was before the experience of the Resurrection. They had only their faith to support them. Desperation must have clung closer to them than their own shadows.

How were they to know that this apparent defeat was a definitive victory?

Of course, we have a faith born after the Resurrection, and can feel less challenged at the foot of the cross, although not always when that cross is our own. Faith born of the Resurrection teaches us that the hour of the cross was the Pyrrhic victory of evil. Pyrrhus was a Greek general, whose defeat of his enemies in a battle in Southern Italy led him to say, "Another such victory, and I will return home alone." A Pyrrhic victory is one that incapacitates the victor.

This is another example of so many paradoxes of Christian faith: the apparent defeat of Jesus on Calvary was actually the failure of evil. The mystical tide was turned in human history. The story of evil since then is evil's retreat from the power of Christ. This retreat is unfortunately like the path of the armies through Russia, with thousands of acres of scorched earth and harvests destroyed in a final destructive frenzy, and many casualties. But it is nevertheless a retreat.

An Irish revolutionary, Terence MacSwiney, unconsciously described the victory of good on the cross of Jesus when he said, "It is not those who can inflict the most, but those that can suffer the most who will conquer." In Jesus' acceptance of suffering we have the victory we need. He was "obedient even to death," the words were written in Latin on the marble above the crucifix of the old chapel of the seminary I attended. How many times did I see that inscription, and yet I rarely considered how obedience also would have a price in my life.

If we could only remember the reflection of Martin Luther King about this: "Unearned suffering is redemptive." The three witnesses saw the greatest of unearned suffering. They had the chance to recognize Jesus' acceptance of it, even if they did not understand it. We should get close to them for a while and think about this Word, so that its profundity and its power can resonate in us and in our lives.

# Mary Magdalene

She obviously did not believe that the Word meant that there would be no more to the story. Her anxiety to go to the tomb cannot have been merely the rites of mourning. Her heart must have known that the story was not finished. How could she merely accept a defeat to her dreams that seemed so terrifying and total?

What would we say at the foot of the cross? Wouldn't we want to say, "No, this cannot be the way it should end! No, we do not accept this!" It must have been hard for Mary Magdalene to console herself at the foot of the cross. Many artists have imagined her weeping dramatically at the foot of the cross. On Easter Sunday, she was still crying. How painful her grief must have been. Love makes us suffer very much for those we love; sometimes it makes us wish to take their pain upon ourselves.

The Resurrection appearance to Mary Magdalene in John 20 gives us some clues about her reaction to this Word. It is so obvious that she was not prepared to accept things as they were. First, she goes to the tomb, in John's version of things, apparently alone. Then she hurries to take the news to the apostles. But after Peter and John are come and gone, she is again in the cemetery. The two apostles do not seem to see her or talk to her, but Jesus himself appears to her.

After the apostles are gone, she enters the scene again. She is still weeping, and then stoops to see in the tomb, just as the Beloved Disciple had a few minutes before. She sees two angels there. The angels ask her why she is weeping. She answers because the Lord has been taken away and then turns to see Jesus, whom she does not recognize. The scene is really special, completely suffused with the supernatural: angels are talking to a saint who is looking for the body of Jesus while He stands behind her.

In this enigmatic encounter, she at first does not recognize the Lord, just like the disciples on the road to Emmaus who would also not recognize Him later that day. She thinks He is the gardener, which makes you wonder how He was dressed, since such workers were always poor, and the poor do not wear fine clothes to work in the dirt. Jesus asks Mary Magdalene the same question as the angels, and then, "Whom do you seek?" This evokes a response from Mary. If He has taken the body of the Lord away, she wants Him to tell her.

She has stopped crying, and is taking an active stance. The change indicates something of her character. The exchange also makes me think that Mary Magdalene was wealthy, as tradition has had it. She has the wealthy woman's take-charge attitude, and is not afraid to tell the man, "I will take care of the body." Since, if the gardener did take the body, it would have been by order of someone else, she is assuming that she could countermand or at least modify such orders. She had not been fazed by the presence of the angels in the tomb and she was not about to let the gardener make her shy.

The irony of the Gospels allows us to wait to see when she will recognize Jesus, just as in a play or a movie we wait to see the truth dawn on a character. Then Jesus says her name. Pope John Paul II recently used this passage as an illustration of his theme of "encounter with Jesus Christ, the way to conversion, communion, and solidarity," in his exhortation *Ecclesia in America*. The communion in this encounter is the brief dialog between the two. He calls her "Mary," and she calls Him "Teacher." Then He says that she should not cling to Him, which is another detail that has been much discussed. Had she embraced Him as though never to let Him go? A commentary in the Latin American Bible says that He says "nole me tangere," to quote it in Latin, because they would "now have a new relationship." That sounds to me like making a virtue of necessity and saying there was a change because something had changed. That has to be some reason, but perhaps it is something simple, like the urgency of the message the Lord gives her.

Jesus had said that everything had been accomplished, but evidently there was something left to be accomplished in Mary Magdalene — her election to be the Apostle of the Apostles, the message bearer of the Risen Lord.

Perhaps that is the insight we can bear from standing near Mary as she hears this Word. The demon of doubt fought faith in her heart, but faith won. She had instinctively, although undoubtedly with confusion and pain, sought out an encounter with the Lord, and had found Him. The change the Lord asks of her, and the solidarity implied in charging her with a mission, are the natural results of her communion with the Lord.

Do you know in your heart that God's will has been accomplished in Jesus? Are you certain of God's desire to save you and that salvation offered you in faith in Jesus? I think one way to test this is to pray, "Lord Jesus, I know that you have accomplished your Father's plan for us, and that what is left for us is that it be accomplished in us. Help me to open myself to that." It is another of the paradoxes in which our faith abounds, "Lord, you have said, 'It is finished.' Now, finish me. Bring me to completion, too."

## The Beloved Disciple

The Gospel of Matthew begins with the genealogy of Jesus reaching back to Abraham. The Gospel of Mark begins with the mission of the Baptist. The Gospel of Luke begins with the annunciation of the birth of John to his father Zechariah. All of these contrast with the beginning of the Gospel of John, which starts before creation in eternity.

This insight of the eternal plan of God is part of the reason that St. John is called the theologian of the evangelists. This plan is given capsule form in the famous dialog with Nicodemus, in which the most memorized quote in the whole Bible is given, "For God so loved the world that he gave his one and only Son, that whoever believes in him shall not perish but have eternal life" ( Jn 3:16).

I think of the Beloved Disciple at the foot of the cross learning the lesson which he would express in his writings with the help of the Holy Spirit. He hears Jesus say that his work is finished, and he tries to understand it. The phrase, "It is finished," begs the elucidation, "What exactly is finished?" I suppose you could take the Words literally as saying no more than that Jesus' life was finished. But the sense of accomplishment, which the Word contains in the original text, must make us look beyond to a deeper meaning.

There was a Mexican revolutionary who said that over his grave people might say either that "he was a dreamer," or that, "he was crazy," but could not say: "Here lies a coward who betrayed his own ideas." I think that the Beloved Disciple appreciated the strength that Jesus showed on the cross. His own bravery as the only man who identified himself with the Crucified One was a reflection of the serenity of his Master in the midst of hatred and hostility.

The poet Ezra Pound has a poem about Jesus called "Ballad of the Goodly Fere" (Fere means "mate" or "companion"). Pound calls Jesus a "man of men," and the ballad celebrates Christ's victory over His enemies. The coolness of Christ in the face of danger is highlighted by this stanza:

> "Ye ha' seen me heal the lame and blind,
> And wake the dead," says he,
> "Ye shall see one thing to master all:
> 'Tis how a brave man dies on the tree."[8]

The Beloved Disciple certainly described the death of a brave man. He could see the calm and the courage in the face of what looked like human tragedy, if not misery. Looking at what others would regard as a shameful fate in the eye and saying, "It is accomplished," is an act of human courage just as it is divine wisdom. The humanity of Jesus showed us how to act. This is one of the central insights of Pope John Paul II: true humanity is what we see in Jesus. This goes against the saying, "To err is human." So many times we define humanity in terms of weakness, and it is certain that sin acts in us as automatically as gravity, as Victor Hugo wrote. However, redeemed humanity, which we can see in Jesus and in Mary, too, is actually the real idea we should have of what being human can mean.

Many authors have commented upon the serenity of Jesus in the passion narrative of the fourth Gospel. Jesus lays down His life to take it up again. He is completely in command, which is obvious from Gethsemane when those seeking Him fall down terror-stricken when He says, "It is I." Hemingway said that heroism was grace under pressure. That definition would make Jesus the archetype of all heroes. His serenity in the face of torture and death is a study in grace for us.

The Beloved Disciple, who was given the opportunity to observe so closely the last moments of Jesus' earthly life, was studying that peace which only his Master knew. I imagine him at the foot of the cross asking himself how Jesus could be so tranquil and what that meant. The reason I think that he was already turning these ideas over in his head is because of the revelation of the empty tomb.

Peter and the Beloved Disciple ran to the tomb together. The second, a younger man, reached the tomb first. He looks in the empty tomb, but does not enter until after Peter. When he did enter, says John 20:8b, "He saw and believed." The Beloved Disciple is thus given the distinction of being the first to believe in the Resurrection, even ahead of Mary Magdalene, who was its messenger. Could this be because the Beloved Disciple had started to study eternity from the foot of the cross?

From all eternity, this had been God's will. The implications of this have been the meditation of the Church for centuries. It means that the Word becoming Flesh was also part of the divine wisdom before time was born. If that is so, our own bodies, sometimes so weak and so ravaged by age and sickness, were part of the plan. The great Fulton Sheen spoke about this truth and used a metaphor borrowed from the art of portrait painting. His premise was that, "From all eternity God willed to make man in the image of His eternal Son." This being so, the Incarnation represents the recuperation of that image. Bishop Sheen continues:

> In some mysterious way the revolt of Lucifer echoed to earth, and the image of God in man was blurred and ruined. . . . In order that the portrait might once more be true to the Original, God willed to send to earth His Divine Son according to whose image man was made, that the earth might see once more the manner of man God wanted us to be.

I have heard of a person who bought a house from a man who was confined to a wheelchair. The house had many special characteristics, including ramps and even light switches that were much below standard height. The dimensions of the house had been tailored to fit the owner. It is a tremendous thought that God shaped man with a similar concern for a model. One of the startling ironics of the Genesis account of God creating Adam out of clay is that the Son of God would join Himself with human flesh.

Divinity looked through eyes like ours. Divinity experienced what it felt like to have an empty stomach. Divinity knew fatigue and the heaviness of arms and legs that it brings. Divinity was no stranger to human emotions and sorrow, even to tears. Divinity had a heart that beat like ours and even ceased to function. Divinity not only breathed but could stop breathing. Divinity could be held as dead weight in the arms of a mother and be buried.

Our Creed tells us that Jesus was both human and divine, and not divided into sections but in a union which is unity. That means: "When God became man, man also became God," as a medieval philosopher wrote. The Beloved Disciple wrote of this in 1 John 3:2: "Dear friends, now we are children of God, and what we will be has not yet been made known. But we know that when he appears, we shall be like him, for we shall see him as he is."

Some scholastic theologians meditated the Incarnation, the Word made into our own flesh and blood, and concluded that it was at the root of the Lucifer's rebellion. The thought that the Son of God would become a creature inferior to the angels, according to this reading, scandalized the Prince of Darkness. How could infinity stoop to the finite, skipping the ranks of the angels? The thought of the jealousy of the angels is certainly provocative juxtaposed with the passion and death of Jesus. It does, however, give us an intuition of the eternal mystery of the Incarnation.

The fourth evangelist saw the worst aspect of the Incarnation. He knew therefore that God could become man and still be rejected, tortured, and killed. He saw the Son of God bow His head and die. But the Beloved Disciple saw the empty tomb and believed. The victim of the execution was He, through whom "all things were made" (Jn 1:3). Creation turned against its creator on Calvary, but He only spoke Words of love to respond to the attack.

The dependence of all creation upon Jesus is the theme of the famous Irish poet Joseph Mary Plunkett, a great patriot who was killed by the British after the Easter uprising. The poem expresses some of the majestic power of the Incarnation, which is certainly congruent to theme of the imperial grace of the Son of God in the fourth Gospel. The poem was once an essential part of American Catholic curriculum but now is unfortunately unknown to many. It is worth remembering and savoring.

## I See His Blood Upon The Rose

I see his blood upon the rose
And in the stars the glory of his eyes,
His body gleams amid eternal snows,
His tears fall from the skies.

I see his face in every flower;
The thunder and the singing of the birds
Are but his voice — and carven by his power
Rocks are his written words.

All pathways by his feet are worn,
His strong heart stirs the ever-beating sea,
His crown of thorns is twined with every thorn,
His cross is every tree.[9]

Next to the Beloved Disciple in the shadow of the cross, we should listen to this Word of Jesus and hear how it echoes in eternity.

## The Blessed Virgin Mary

She had been told at the beginning how much God had loved her. "You will be with child and give birth to a son, and you are to give him the name Jesus. He will be great and will be called the Son of the Most High. The Lord God will give him the throne of his father David, and he will reign over the house of Jacob forever; his kingdom will never end" (Lk 1:31-33).

The contrast of the words of the Annunciation with the reality of Calvary had to be heartbreaking. The only references to royalty were the mockery of the scroll hung over the cross, the perverse jest of the thorns twisted into a crown, and the insults of the soldiers and the crowd of enemies.

She had sung in the Magnificat: "He has performed mighty deeds with his arm, he has scattered those who are proud in their inmost thoughts. / He has brought down rulers from their thrones, but has lifted up the humble. / He has filled the hungry with good things but has sent the rich away empty" (Lk 1:51-53).

All of this would seem to be negated by the crucifixion. How could this poor woman, who had been so hopeful, bear this loss? She had not had an easy life, for all the talk of thrones. She had known the terror of flight and the stress of exile. The obscurity of Nazareth had been peaceful, but that peace had been under a sword of Damocles, the prophecies of Simeon about her son. The tempestuous public ministry of Jesus had followed, and she must have had doubts and fears about how it would all end for Him. Even the miracles, which pleased the people so much, were provocations to the reign of terror of the Roman occupation.

The welcome to Jerusalem must have seemed a dream, but how quickly it had turned to nightmare. Who like Mary could have felt the hatred in the air as Jesus was condemned and marched off to die? Who could have felt in her soul as much as she the insults and the pain that He suffered on the cross?

And now she hears that it has all been according to plan. Obviously the words of Simeon had to echo in her heart: "This child is destined to cause the falling and rising of many in Israel, and to be a sign that will be spoken against, so that the thoughts of many hearts will be revealed. And a sword will pierce your own soul, too" (Lk 2:34-35).

Even this prophecy had proved too optimistic, she might have thought. Where were the many rising in Israel? The thoughts of many hearts had proved ugly thoughts indeed, thoughts of violence and hatred. The part about the sword rang true, however, because this was cutting right through to her heart.

Was this what God had wanted? Her special vocation had been one of isolation. With reason the Gospel says that she "stored these things in her heart," because what else could she have done with them? As one of the faithful people of Israel, she must have had a share of Messianic expectation, also. Weren't her hopes dashed along with all the rest?

Some great artists have shown Mary in complete weakness at the foot of the cross. She was the archetype of the mother mourning her children, the portrait of grief past grief. Other artists, however, including Michelangelo, show a serene Mary. The Pietà, after all, is a sculpture of Mary at the worst point in her life, and yet she does not seem uncontrollably sad.

I would side with Michelangelo in this respect. I believe Mary could have been collected even in her grief. I say this because of another woman I know. She is a member of one of the prayer groups in the parish. Not long ago, we were reflecting on the faith in the will of God, and she was moved to tell her story.

She lives in a small town a few kilometers from the seashore. Her son decided to go to the beach one day as a kind of an excursion. She was invited, but had decided to go to Mass instead. There was only one Mass in the small town, and that about midday. Her son had been in a good mood, she remembered, and she had said, "Have a good time."

Later in the afternoon, she had heard that there had been a shooting at the beach. A neighbor had asked her if she knew that two men had been drinking and that one had shot and killed the other. The neighbor did not know who the victim was, but the mother instantly felt that the dead man was her son. "May God be blessed," she said, echoing old prayers, "I commended him to God and to the Blessed Virgin, and prayed for forgiveness for the one who killed him."

I wish I could describe the way the woman talked about this. Her voice was calm, although she talked in very low tones. As she spoke, it seemed as though she was reliving what had happened on that day. She had a faraway look in her eyes, and she spoke almost without taking a breath, as if she had said it all before many times or maybe because she wanted to say it all at once. It was clear that it was all still painful to her, but also that she harbored no resentments about anything. This had happened to her, she would never forget it, but she would not hate, either.

If this woman could have the grace and presence of mind to pray even for her son's killer, why couldn't Mary? The special grace of this Salvadoran woman was that vengeance killings are a reality in this country. Her spirit of forgiveness was like a block for what could have been a chain of deaths. "They couldn't give him back to me," she said, "what else could I do but pray to God?"

"Every son receives from his mother," said Hans Urs von Balthasar in a meditation on Mary as the New Eve (*Elucidations*, Ignatius, p.108). One of the things that Jesus received was the silent witness of love on Calvary. I am sure that even there she was always the Handmaid of the Lord. Even there, she had to be open to His will, just as she was when she said, "Let it be done to me according to thy word" to the angel at the Annunciation.

This is not to discount how much it must have cost her. For us to say we are heartbroken is not the same thing as to talk about a heart as fine and holy as hers being torn apart. But even this pain went to the treasury of her soul. Many times we use Job as an example of patience, and yet at one point he asks to see God in what could sound like impatience. Mary is a much greater example of patience because she had known that suffering would come, even though she did not know what shape it would take.

She had been troubled by the greeting of the angel, and then puzzled about his message. Is it too much to think that her heart harked back to that first call to accept God's will? Wasn't this the bitterest of accomplishments? What but pure faith could have sustained her in the hour of the death of her Son?

If we could have looked into her eyes at that hour, what would we have seen? We are accustomed to seeing her in paintings and holy cards with a reflection of the bliss in heaven, with halos and holy joy painted in vivid colors. How many crowns she now wears in images, who never imagined wearing one in life? What would her eyes have told us?

I think they would have said to us that she suffered, but that she believed. She loved. What more would we want to learn from her? Through it all, she accepted God's will and loved. At her side, can we question this Word of fulfillment? Our own doubts should take shame when confronted with her faith.

## Conclusion

Again the three witnesses have helped us to hear a Word of Jesus from the cross. Now we have to make our own response to the invitation it represents. An older style of piety talked about conformity to the will of God. We are now more inclined to think about our rights than to consider that God will might be something difficult for us.

Blessed Josémaria Escrivá, a man who had more than his share of misunderstanding by others in the Church, meditated much about the will of God. He has this to say about troubles, from his book *The Way*:

> Are you suffering some great tribulation? Do you have reverses? Say very slowly, as if savoring the words, this powerful and manly prayer: "May the most just and lovable will of God be done, be fulfilled, be praised and eternally exalted above all things. Amen, Amen." I assure you that you'll find peace (*Camino*, 691).

Jesus was recognizing that He had completed His mission when He said this Word. The same Word should make us wish to do the same. We should pray about the mystery that is the will of God for each one of us, our special vocation and participation in God's plan for the redemption of the world. "Make me a heart," says a hymn in Spanish, "which loves greatly." Such a heart would be like that of the man on the cross.

## Prayer

*Jesus on the cross, I love You.*

*Give me the courage to hear this Word. Help me to desire more than anything to do the will of Your Father. Give me the courage that I need, and the patience, to model my life on Your suffering wisdom.*

*Let God's will be accomplished in me, too. Amen.*

# CHAPTER SEVEN

# The Seventh Word

*It was now about the sixth hour, and darkness came over the whole land until the ninth hour, for the sun stopped shining. And the curtain of the temple was torn in two. Jesus called out with a loud voice, "Father, into your hands, I commit my spirit." When he had said this, he breathed his last (Lk 23:44-46).*

For a second time, Jesus quotes a psalm from the cross. This time it is Psalm 31, and it is not the first verse but the fifth. The Book of Psalms was the hymnal of the pious Jew, and so it is appropriate that its cadences and phrases would be part of Jesus' prayer. In this case, Jesus modifies the verse by directing it to the Father. This is interesting as a sign of the unity of the Old and New Testaments. The psalm was originally addressed to "Yahweh" and Jesus indicates by this simple prayer that the God of the fathers is His Father.

The synthesis of the two covenants reminds us that the Church has always read the psalms from the point of view of Christ. That is the reason why the Liturgy of the Hours is the official prayer of the Church. Some of the recent controversy about the translation of the psalms into English was concern about losing the specific Christological meaning that the Church applies to the psalms. The insight that must be preserved is that *the* Word of God is a unity. Hans Urs von Balthasar summarized this by saying that every part of the Word was somehow about the Word, that all Scripture is about Jesus Christ the definitive Word of God to the human race.

In this case, the Word is citing the Word, and so we need to look at Psalm 31 to try to understand why Jesus saw this particular psalm as a means of expressing what He was experiencing in his final moments. Psalm 31 is actually a song of thanksgiving, expressing gratitude for the Lord's help in persecution and sickness. The prayer of the psalm recalls both the plots of his enemies and physical suffering, two notes obviously very evident in Calvary.

The great Bible scholar Father Luis Alonso Schokel saw the structure of this psalm as a kind of legal brief directed to God, the just Judge. He said that the psalmist in his suffering is calling on God to notice his faith and help him escape from the trap set by his enemies. Despite his troubles, he feels secure in the Lord's protection.

As with Psalm 22, it is easy to see the connection between what is happening to Jesus on Calvary and the prayer on his lips. The parallel with Jesus' suffering on the cross is both physical and emotional. The psalmist is suffering terribly. This is expressed in his body by physical pain, a pain so intense that he weeps so much "his eyes grow weak" and makes him "groan" and feel completely weak. In his spirit, he suffers because he is abandoned by those close to him, including friends and neighbors. People avoid him when they see him on the street; he is forgotten as if he were dead; he is mocked and his name is used as slander. Besides this, from his former friends and acquaintances, there are others who conspire against him and plot his death.

Schokel makes an interesting point about the word translated here as "commit" and often as "commend." The word comes from the vocabulary of commerce or business. Another use of the same word in the Bible is in the Book of Tobit, where it refers to the money deposited with a certain Gabael, for which the father of Tobiah had a receipt that was twenty years old. The language is contractual, which seems unusual in prayer, but is useful because it emphasizes a kind of mutuality, and the expectation of the recuperation of what is deposited.

Thus Jesus is "depositing" his spirit, "principle of life" in the "hands" of God (the original Hebrew had only the singular, *hand*). The implication of this language is that what is "deposited" is safe, and that it will be possible to get it back again. By quoting the psalm, Jesus is not only making reference to his circumstances, his physical and emotional suffering, but is also expressing his characteristic stance of security in the love of his Father.

Father Schokel sees a reference in the verse, "My times are in your hands," to Ecclesiastes, chapter three which talks about the cycles of life, a time for being born and for dying, for crying and laughing, for keeping silence and talking, etc. All these times are in the hands of God, meaning that our whole existence is within the experience of the love of God. Jesus, by referring to this psalm, is juxtaposing his sacrificial death with the message with which the psalm concludes, "Be strong and take heart, all you who hope in the LORD" (Ps 31:24).

I realize that the discussion might appear technical to some, with references to ancient customs and particular words. Some Scripture study requires patience because it is a little like panning for gold nuggets from a stream. The reward of this labor leads us to understand that in the last moment of His life, when all seemed to be lost, Jesus repeated His confidence. He was teaching us to never forget that God is our Father and in Him we have security.

This Last Word of Jesus is clearly a model. We can see its echo in the last words of St. Stephen in the Acts of the Apostles: "While they were stoning him, Stephen prayed, 'Lord Jesus, receive my spirit.' Then he fell on his knees and cried out, 'Lord, do not hold this sin against them.' When he had said this, he fell asleep" (Acts 7:59-60).

The death of Stephen is the first Christian death after Jesus, and is very much an imitation of the same. The saint's last words reflect the model of Christ on the cross, not only in his confidence but also in his sense of witness to his persecutors. Stephen's words are a last testament, a model of faith in Jesus, and a spirit of forgiveness. Where Jesus invoked the Father, Stephen invokes Christ, while at the same time pleading for his enemies.

The model has been followed by saints through the ages. It is a Christian and pious wish to die reconciled, not only with one's friends and family, but even and especially with one's enemies. I have found consciousness of this in some of the simplest of God's people. It is always edifying to see that someone in the last moments of life is aware of the need to forgive. We should all pray to have that kind of grace and clarity. Unfortunately, there are counter examples of people who seem to carry their resentments to their graves.

I suppose it sounds a bit morbid to some, but I wonder if we should not think of a prayer which we should like to have on our lips at the final hour. It would be a tremendous grace to be able to leave an example for others, words that would inspire faith in others.

This will to make a statement or set an example reminds me of the ironic humor of the last words of Pancho Villa, the Mexican bandit turned general of the Revolution. He was something of a historical figure, famous for evading the U.S. Army under General Pershing who had made an over-the-border raid, and perhaps was aware of his status. Pancho Villa apparently wanted to say something memorable in the last moment, but couldn't think of anything. Just before the shots rang out, he said, "Don't let it end like this. Tell them that I said something."

The Lord did not have Pancho Villa's problem, as this book bears testimony. Jesus' Last Words are a prayer, and an expression of complete confidence in God the Father. The Gospel of Luke says that Jesus cried out in a loud voice so that everyone present could hear this final Word. Did they console the witnesses?

## Mary Magdalene

Perhaps one of Mary Magdalene's demons was a lack of confidence in God. I can imagine what she feels as she hears Jesus, not only calling God His Father, but also expressing absolute trust in Him. If she was a wealthy person, as tradition implies, she would know about deposits of money. Luke, chapter eight, says that Mary Magdalene was among the group of women, including Susanna, the wife of Herod's steward, who provided for Jesus and his disciples, "out of their means."

Was this work in "administration" part of her former life, which was useful in her discipleship? I like to think of Mary Magdalene as a take-charge person, a woman who knew the ways of the world. We have already seen her attitude with the supposed gardener near the tomb of Jesus. She would know where to deposit her money in that case. Perhaps what would have been lacking to her would have been a corresponding security in spiritual matters.

And would she know God as Father, too? She has not been called so, but tradition really has profiled Mary Magdalene as a kind of prodigal daughter. Taking her as a symbol of conversion, as tradition has always done, we can also say that she gives example of reconciliation with God the Father. That mercy had come to her because of her relationship with Jesus.

Her experience of Jesus was that of real discipleship, personal conversion, what the Bible calls *metanoia*,[10] and then follow-up formation. Mary Magdalene was one of those who followed the Lord from what had to be the heady days of Galilee to the heartbreak of Jerusalem. She had seen some of the trajectory of the Preacher whose career in terms of the public must have been like a comet, of rapid appearance and disappearance, but also something dramatic and very moving.

As one who was close to Jesus, she must have heard Him talking about the love of His Father. When the angels talk to her and to the other women "who had come from Galilee" in the Resurrection appearance in Luke's Gospel, they are at pains to remind them, "how he told you, while he was still with you in Galilee: The Son of Man must be delivered into the hands of sinful men, be crucified and on the third day be raised again" (Lk 24:6-7). The Gospel then says that they "remembered," implying that they should have known because they had been told.

If that were so, the Last Words of Jesus would be like a final exam for Mary Magdalene. They represent all that Jesus had intended to do and to teach. How could she respond to it? I think that perhaps the first thing in her mind would be how she related to Jesus. Many women think in terms of their relationships and seek clarity in them where men might ignore interpersonal dynamics and be only concerned about objective as opposed to subjective experience.

Did her thoughts go to how her relationship with Jesus had changed her life? There is a poem of the Irish poet Yeats that represents a kind of time capsule commentary on a relationship. Entitled "When You Are Old," it is based upon a French poem predicting that a lover would regret her rejection of the poet. However, Yeats' sonnet is full of nostalgia and lost possibility, not remembered in terms of an emotional revenge, as in the French poem, but as a kind of tragedy. The middle stanza expresses the love that the poet had for the woman, and I have always thought it is a spiritual love. It could even express how the Lord loved Mary Magdalene:

> How many loved your moments of glad grace,
> And loved your beauty with a love false or true.
> But one man loved the pilgrim soul of you,
> And loved the sorrows of your changing face.

Jesus had loved the pilgrim soul in Mary Magdalene. No one had ever been so aware of all her needs before. No one, perhaps, had called forth such a response from her. Her courage at the tomb should indicate to us Mary Magdalene's commitment to Jesus. She was ready to fight for a decent burial for Him, certainly a symbolic activity, like most of our funerals. Jesus had loved her for who she was in the eyes of God. She could not let go of that. She could not pretend to go on as before.

No wonder she was so upset on Easter Sunday. I imagine her weeping uncontrollably. Her tears seem to have frightened the angels, who asked her why she was crying, and made Christ appear to her. She did not understand all that Jesus had implied in his Last Words. In fact, she was confused by what had happened and was trying to impose order on it, if only in locating where the Body of Jesus had been placed. Her reaction was not the perfect mirror of faith, but it was an index of love. That is why she is important to us: she shows us growth in faith. She was present for both mysteries, the cross and the Resurrection. The continuity of the story in her personal history delineates a path for us.

We are trying to place ourselves with the three witnesses in the moment of the Word to try to receive the Words with the love that they did. We have an advantage over the witnesses, however, in seeing beyond to the Resurrection. However, they continued to grow. Especially with Mary Magdalene we have been aware of her role as a witness of both the cross and the Resurrection.

Working my way through these meditations, I have felt that Mary Magdalene was more like most of us than either the Beloved Disciple or the Blessed Virgin Mary. Perhaps ignorance makes me bold in this, because we really know so much about her. But there is also the fact that we can see her relating to John and Mary and representing us sinners.

Maybe we have not had seven demons expelled from us, but most of us have felt some experience of failure in our relationship with God. Most of us have felt that we have experienced change in our relationship with Jesus, including changes that had to do with our own lack of faith. Perhaps the attractiveness of some of the Resurrection narratives for us is that we can appreciate the sharp turn away from despair that comes when Jesus says the name of His disciple and she recognizes Him.

Even her presumed over-reaction ("Do not cling to me," says Jesus) might sound like something we could fall into. The stories of her life of penitence after the Resurrection might not impress us as something worthy of emulation, but the perseverance implied is an undeniable Christian ideal.

Mary Magdalene was part of the story of the rock opera *Jesus Christ, Superstar*, and her song in that popular oratorio was "I don't know how to love him." This pretended to address a feeling of conflict she had about her feelings about Jesus which certainly reflected more about our culture than the biblical figure, but still indicates the attractiveness of the saint as a symbol. Other avatars of Mary Magdalene in movies have been less respectful, however, but obviously our culture has a problem with understanding the motivation of saints.

I think, however, that all of us can see her as a pilgrim soul. Mary Magdalene stands for all of us at the foot of the cross. Her personal struggle to find hope and peace in Jesus is more obvious than that of the Beloved Disciple or of the Blessed Virgin Mary. We should identify with her precisely because we can relate to how difficult it all must have been for her.

The drama of her hearing the Last Word is the drama of encounter with Jesus that leads to faith and it is our drama, also. The obvious stages of her discipleship: before conversion; before Calvary; after Calvary; and after the Resurrection, serves as a pattern for must of us who grow in stages, slowly and sometimes painfully.

Imagining her struggling to accept this Last Word of Jesus with its implied intimacy with the Father and its wagering all on God's good will, has made me feel less alone in my own struggle for faith. We can identify with a person who has struggled and has grown. We are in good company with her at the foot of the cross.

## The Beloved Disciple

He would later be the evangelist who most tried to reveal the relationship between Father and Son. This Last Word of confidence in the Father is completely congruent with his Gospel of the love between the first two Persons in God.

The Beloved Disciple became the mystic poet of the love of Father and Son. This is obvious even from a casual reading of the fourth Gospel. When St. Thomas says with customary bravery that the apostles are not certain about where Jesus is headed, Jesus responds to him:

> I am the way and the truth and the life. No one
> comes to the Father except through me. If you re-
> ally knew me, you would know my Father as well.

From now on, you do know him and have seen
him (Jn 14:6-7).

The Beloved Disciple indicates that even after this statement,
Philip is not sure, and asks to see the Father.

Jesus answered, "Don't you know me, Philip, even
after I have been among you such a long time?
Anyone who has seen me has seen the Father. How
can you say, "Show us the Father"? Don't you believe that I am in the Father, and that the Father is
in me? The words I say to you are not just my own.
Rather, it is the Father, living in me, who is doing
his work. Believe me when I say that I am in the
Father and the Father is in me; or at least believe
on the evidence of the miracles themselves (Jn
14:9-11).

A real student studies his teacher and gets to think like him. I
imagine John taking in all that Jesus said about his Father, and all
that had happened, and trying to express it so that others could understand. The language of the fourth Gospel is elliptical sometimes
and there are many repetitions. I think that is because the Beloved
Disciple always wanted to come to home base. The ultimate point of
reference was the love of the Father, which Jesus was and taught.

This was not a fact to be narrated, like an event or a special
saying. It was a reality that the believer was invited to live. That was
why God's love had to be repeatedly expressed, to convince the believer to enter into it as a dimension of existence. The relationship
between Father and Son was not something just about Jesus. It was
something offered to the follower of Jesus.

If anyone loves me, he will obey my teaching. My
Father will love him, and we will come to him and
make our home with him (Jn 14:23).

This is one verse in the Gospel, but it is a world of meaning.
That is the meaning which the Beloved Disciple was absorbing at
the foot of the cross, which he saw in the empty tomb, and which he
recognized on the shores of the Sea of Galilee.

The Beloved Disciple eventually knew that all of us had to say
"Father" to God, just as Christ did in this last of the Last Words. He
eventually knew that the handing-over to God expressed in committing or commending your spirit to Him was something for every
Christian.

Not all the Words from the cross can be put into our lives as
easily as this last one. We might not be able to say, "Father, forgive
them, for they know not what they do," with complete sincerity. We
certainly are not able to promise: "This day you will be with me in
paradise," nor "Woman, behold your son." We can and do say, however, that we feel abandoned sometimes by God, even forsaken. We
are able to say with Jesus, "I thirst," even if we cannot enter into all
that He signified by that. We could say, "It is finished," some day, if
our souls are prepared for it.

The easiest of these saying to put on our own lips, however, is,
"Father, into your hands I commit my spirit." We can call God Father, the most extraordinary kind of declaration of intimacy. And we
can wager our lives on God. I think that is what the Beloved Disciple would try to work out for himself and for us, who depend on
him so much for the portrait of our Lord.

He must have known the psalm, perhaps even before he became
a member of the disciples of Jesus. He probably, however, had heard
Jesus say this psalm in another context, the prayer of the disciples.

Thus he could make a connection between the prayer of Jesus in the sense of the Lord's spirituality and the last prayer Jesus said in this life. The Beloved Disciple would know that the last prayer was a model for us. Standing next to him as he looks up to his Lord on the cross, we should try to repeat the Words of Jesus and make them our own.

## The Blessed Virgin Mary

Did she remember another uncomfortable hour in which He also had invoked His father? He had been a child of twelve years, still too young for His bar mitzvah. (Although He was not a "son of the covenant.") He had gone missing in Jerusalem during their yearly pilgrimage at Passover. In fact, the child lost and found is a small version of the Passover, with reference both to the last plague of Egypt, which menaced the first-born, and even a hint of resurrection, in the appearance on the third day. It was after three days that they found Jesus in the Temple, three days in which both she and Joseph had perhaps contemplated the possibility that He had been sold into slavery like the other beloved son of the Bible or even that He was no longer alive.

There He was among the teachers of the Temple, asking them penetrating questions. Mary and Joseph were "astonished" says Luke. But Mary does not hesitate to ask, "Son, why have you treated us like this? Your father and I have been anxiously searching for you" (Lk 2:48).

This sounds hasty, even blurted out, especially since it has for an audience the solemn group of admiring scholars. "How could you do this?" is the expression of someone who is wounded, who expects better of the other person. Certainly it indicates that the carelessness of Jesus seemed a betrayal to Mary. She is hurt and not only not intimidated by the others present, but also is not distracted by the fact that Jesus is impressing these important men, something which might have disarmed another mother. The first thing she does is reprimand Him. Even though it takes place in Jerusalem in the center of worship of the Jewish people, this is very much a domestic scene, like so many misunderstandings from our own childhood.

Of further interest is how Mary includes Joseph in the scene. The patriarch is silent, but Mary says "your father and I" and indicates that he was anxious, also, about the adopted son. This is a portrait of a family, just like those diagrams that some family counselors use to indicate relationships. Mary wants the child to know that not only she but also Joseph has been looking for Him desperately. It is an inclusive note, typically feminine and maternal.

Jesus does not seem to react to her hurt, although what He said could be expressed in any number of tones. He says to her, "Why were you looking for me? Did you not know that it was necessary that I be in the things of my Father?" I cannot help feeling that this answer was more terrifying than the three days without Him, because it implied a vision of the future in which Jesus' vocation would steadily separate Him from the life of Nazareth.

What is translated in the version the Bible I am using as "the house of my Father" is the Greek word "things." For that reason, there is the other interpretation, "my Father's business." However it is translated, the response represents that what He was about was not the same as His day-to-day life in Nazareth. First of all, Mary and Jesus use "father" in two different ways, referring to two different people. She says your " father" was anxious, Jesus says that He had to be about the business of His Father. She has expressed surprise, and He is surprised right back, because He thinks that His vocation should be obvious to her. What surprises the reader is that all three return to Galilee as if nothing had happened.

Now, at the foot of the cross, there has been much more about the Father. At this time, she has to see herself in the eyes of her Son. She, too, is a daughter. When praying the Rosary in Spanish, the three Hail Mary's, which in English are recited at the beginning asking for an increase in Faith, Hope, and Charity, are said at the end. Usually, they are introduced with a phrase relating Mary to the Blessed Trinity.

"Hail Mary, Daughter of God the Father," "Hail Mary, Mother of God the Son," "Hail Mary, Spouse of the Holy Spirit," begin the prayers. Mary models for us the Trinitarian life of the soul. All of us are related to the Blessed Trinity. The grace of the three persons operates in each of the baptized.

This makes me think of the relationship of Mary to the Blessed Trinity right there at the foot of the cross. Listening to Jesus say this last prayer, could Mary repeat it for herself? This is something we cannot know, obviously. But she was the first one to believe in Jesus because of the message of the angel. Elizabeth hails her as "blessed is the one who has believed the word of God." The faith of Mary must have been confused at times, but it was always an undeniable dimension in her life.

Did she remember her faith before Jesus? She was going to be alone now more than ever. It would be hard to imagine the pain of her separation from Jesus. What panic it gives us sometimes to be separated from people who mean a great deal to us. How hard it is to think that we will have to get along without the consolation or the counsel of those who have meant much to us. Who could have consoled Mary for the loss of Jesus?

What were her thoughts? So these were the things of His Father? Did she look back at a life in which she had always been waiting for some ultimate revelation, always with the sharp pain of wondering what it all could mean? Did she regret anything? If she could choose to do so, would she have chosen this? Even knowing this end?

Was His Father, her Father, too? This is obvious, but of value for us because Mary is model for us. Is God Father for me? Is He for you? The thought of Mary saying that she, too, committed her spirit to God the Father, putting her life in His hands, also, is consoling for me. I believe that Mary was given that grace of praying along with Jesus. In my own circumstances, I want to do the same.

I want to stand next to her. I want to see her lips move as she repeats the Words and as they sink into her soul. I want to be part of her experience of Jesus because I do not have confidence in doing it alone. In the country where I live, we are in the throes of a new Protestant Reformation. It is common to hear preachers say, "I need only Jesus," or, about the mother of Jesus, "That woman still lies in the grave awaiting judgement, why pray to her?" I cannot see the possibility of ignoring Mary and still being close to Jesus.

Partly this is human intuition. Could I have a friend who disliked or ignored my mother? But this is also a theological issue for me. I do not think we ever are alone in our relationship to Jesus. We are always connected to so many others, and that connection is not a burden or an obstacle but a way to life. For me, relationship to Mary is part of my relationship to Christ.

Following the path of these meditations has deepened my awareness of this. I want to be at the foot of the cross, as near to Jesus as I can be. However, I know that I could not do it alone. I have needed to stand near all three witnesses, and have profited from their closeness, but how much Mary has given me. My life with Christ would be so poor without her. I find that it is hard for me to write a conclusion because I do not want to leave her there at the foot of the cross.

Obviously, she is not there suffering. Jesus is in glory and has glorified her, also. But in some sense, as long as our history continues and eternity has not been fully realized in us, Jesus remains on the cross. He suffers with us when we suffer. He is still speaking to us, still teaching us, still offering us His love. The reality of the Resurrection only makes more important that we listen to Him and accept Him. As long as the drama of salvation lasts, we are all still at the foot of the cross. We will be hearing each of these Words from the cross until Christ calls our name.

## Conclusion

A deposit is insured so that we can always come back for it. Jesus commended His spirit to the Father with a notion of security. The commercial vocabulary of the psalm is a hint at resurrection. His life was safe in the hands of His Father. He would "lose" His life only to find it again. He died confident in the love of His Father. Even in the ugliness of Calvary there was that beauty.

Shakespeare has a famous line in *Hamlet*, "The rest is silence." That is not the case here. Even after His dying Words, there were others. For forty days He appeared to His disciples and spoke to them and taught them again what He had tried to before it had all happened. If in Jesus we know that "God speaks," we also know that He is generous with communication. The Resurrection appearances end with St. Paul, who makes a list of all those who were able to experience the Risen Lord. It reminds me of Ezra Pound's poetic formulation in "The Goodly Fere": "I ha' seen him eat of the honeycomb, sin they nailed him to the tree."

Jesus was silent for a little while, and then spoke again. For Mary Magdalene, the silence of Calvary was broken when Jesus asked her why she was crying and then said her name. For the Beloved Disciple it was broken by the Words, "Peace be with you," with which Jesus greeted his apostles Easter Sunday evening. What was there for the Blessed Virgin Mary?

St. Ignatius of Loyola imagines the Resurrection encounter between Mary and Jesus as part of his *Spiritual Exercises*. It is too hard for me to imagine. I think even the Beloved Disciple would have trouble describing the exchange between the two. What I wonder about is whether they even said any words.

## Prayer

*Jesus on the cross, I love You.*

*Let me listen to this Word and all Your Words with the concentration of my heart. You entrusted Yourself to Your Father; help me to do the same. Be patient with me as I try to put in practice Your wisdom from the cross.*

*Along with You, I place myself in the hands of God. Amen.*

# EPILOGUE

■■■■■ ■■■■■■■■ ■■■ ■■■■■■■■■ ■■■■■■■

# The Cross in Your Heart

*These things happened so that the scripture would be fulfilled: "Not one of his bones will be broken," and, as another scripture says, "They will look on the one they have pierced" (Jn 19:36-37).*

I finish these reflections on the anniversary of my ordination to the priesthood. The coincidence makes me both grateful and a bit humbled. It reminds me that my work as a priest and my work with the pen draw from the same well, my vocation to the pastoral care of God's people.

Priesthood is an extroverted ministry; at least that has been my experience as a diocesan priest. It is all about relationships with people both in community and individually. Sometimes one is tempted to try to do some kind of measurement of ministry in terms of concrete achievements, and I am fighting off such a temptation today.

I have criticized some of my brothers in the diocesan clergy for having what I call an "edifice" complex and losing sight of the hidden and spiritual side of ministry in brick-and-mortar monuments. They could probably wonder something similar about writing books.

Constructing parish buildings and writing books have something in common. The intention of both is to make a place of encounter with the Lord. Neither buildings nor books, however, can guarantee that a person will meet the Lord or even pause to think of Him.

There is a comparison of two Greek orators that I think is valuable for preachers. One orator was a magician with words and left the people spellbound when he spoke. They said after his discourse, "How well he spoke." When the other was finished, however, they said, "Let us march." Obviously, every preacher desires to be like the second orator. In my case, in these reflections, I want you to hear the Words of Jesus from the cross spoken to you and that you "look on the one they have pierced."

Recently someone gave me a book of prayers in which I found quoted a stanza from Angelus Sibelius:

> The cross on Golgotha
> Will never save thy soul.
> The cross in thine own heart
> Alone can make thee whole.[11]

Hearing the Last Words of Jesus can put the cross in your heart. My prayer for you is that you have an inner experience of the saving love of Our Lord. I hope that you will be able to listen with your heart to the Words He spoke with His dying breath. They were Words for you and for me.

# Notes

1. *Cathedra* means chair, referring to a place of authority from which a ruler or teacher taught. Cathedral, the name of the church where a bishop resides, is derived from the word referring to the Bishop's chair from which he officially teaches as a bishop.

2. Hail Holy Queen.

3. *St. John Chrysostom: Commentary on St. John the Apostle and Evangelist Homilies 48-88,* translated by Sr. Thomas Aquinas Goggin, S.C.II, New York, Fathers of the Church, Inc., 1960, p. 431.

4. *Auden: In Memory of W.B. Yeats.*

5. *St. John Chrysostom: Commentary on Saint John the Apostle and Evangelist, Homilies 48-88*, translated by Sr. Thomas Aquinas Goggin, S.C.H., New York, Fathers of the Church, Inc., 1960, p. 434.

6. *The Pocket Book of Modern Verse* Oscar Williams, ed., revised third edition by Hyman J. Sobiloff, Pocket Books, division of Simon Schuster, 1972, pp. 449-450.

7. Jacobus de Voragine *The Golden Legend,* translator William Granger Ryan, Princeton University Press, 1993, p. 375.

8. Ezra Pound, *Selected Poems of Ezra Pound*, New Directions, 1957.

9. *The Mentor Book of Irish Poetry*, Devin Garrity, editor, New American Library, 1965, p.324.

10. *Metanoia,* a Greek word literally means to "turn around"; the early Church used the word as a sign that someone who had converted to Christ no longer followed one's own self-interest but rather changed one's direction to follow Christ.

11. *The Edge of Glory: Prayers in the Celtic Tradition* by David Adam, Morehouse Publishing.

# About the Author

Father Richard C. Antall is a priest in the Archdiocese of Cleveland. He is currently serving as a missionary in El Salvador. An award-winning author and columnist, his first book, **The Way of Compassion,** was published in 1997.

Also by Father Richard C. Antall

# The Way of Compassion

Gain strength and courage by meditating on the meaning of the experiences of seven contemporary women through the Church's tradition of the Seven Sorrows of Mary.

0 87973-**854**-5, paper, $8.95, 144 pages

## Our Sunday Visitor 1-800-348-2440
### or http://www.osv.com

Prices and availability of books subject to change without notice.

Our Sunday Visitor...
# *Your Source for Discovering the Riches of the Catholic Faith*

Our Sunday Visitor has an extensive line of materials for young children, teens, and adults. Our books, Bibles, booklets, CD-ROMs, audios, and videos are available in bookstores worldwide.

To receive a FREE full-line catalog or for more information, call **Our Sunday Visitor** at **1-800-348-2440**. Or write, **Our Sunday Visitor** / 200 Noll Plaza / Huntington, IN 46750.

------------------------------------------------------------

Please send me: __ A catalog
Please send me materials on:
   __ Apologetics and catechetics   __ Reference works
   __ Prayer books   __ Heritage and the saints
   __ The family   __ The parish

Name_____

Address_____Apt._____

City_____State___Zip_____

Telephone (   )_____
A93BBABP

------------------------------------------------------------

Please send a friend: __ A catalog
Please send a friend materials on:
   __ Apologetics and catechetics   __ Reference works
   __ Prayer books   __ Heritage and the saints
   __ The family   __ The parish

Name_____

Address_____Apt._____

City_____State___Zip_____

Telephone (   )_____
A93BBABP

------------------------------------------------------------

**Our Sunday Visitor**
200 Noll Plaza
Huntington, IN 46750
**1-800-348-2440**
osvbooks@osv.com

*Your Source for Discovering the Riches of the Catholic Faith*